Raising c

Bring out the best ... your ...

Raising children with virtues

Bring out the best in your child and yourself

Annelies Wiersma

Illustrated by Carlien Dubben

Inspired by the FAMILY VIRTUES GUIDE
by Linda Kavelin Popov
with Dan Popov and John Kavelin

2010 - ACT on Virtues - Groningen - the Netherlands

COPYRIGHT

ISBN/EAN: 978-90-812238-6-7
NUR 854; Key words: education of children and youth
Dutch edition, 1st print November 2007
2nd completely revised print June 2008

Copyright © Annelies Wiersma
Publisher: ACT on Virtues
Illustrations: Carlien Dubben
Cover design: Ineke Broerse & Sander Zoutman
Translation: Ineke Gijsbers and Charles Lips

Annelies Wiersma
FD Rooseveltsraat 29
9728RV Groningen
The Netherlands
(+0031)(0)50-5279139
info@actonvirtues.nl
www.actonvirtues.nl

The virtues are our treasures,
deeply hidden
within us all.
Some are easily visible,
they are part of our character.
Other virtues we practice,
but not yet as well as we could.
And some… are waiting deep within,
perhaps all the way down.
Like a diamond to be found.
Bring it up to the light
and polish all its facets.

Contents:

Foreword

What do all parents want for their children? For them to be happy and for them to be good. The two are deeply connected, because a good character leads to a positive destiny. Every parent also needs tools to bring out the best in each child - to awaken their kindness, respect, flexibility, compassion, and even their joy.

Annelies Wiersma offers the honest, open perspective of a mother applying the tools and strategies of The Virtues Project and my book, *The Family Virtues Guide* to make them deeply useful and totally accessible in everyday life.

I heartily recommend that all parents read her book and enjoy her insights, her humour, and her practical wisdom.

Linda Kavelin Popov,
Co-founder of the Virtues Project

Preface

From the very first moment a child lies in the cradle, a parent wants only one thing: for the child to be happy. But how do you make that happen? How do you get a child ready to step into the world happy, cheerful and confident?

My son Daniel who is eleven now, will soon make the jump to junior high school. His teacher wrote in his last report: "Daniel is a very outgoing and cheerful boy in the class and has many friends. He likes making jokes but also has a good sense for when to stop. He works well in groups and is always ready to help others. He also enjoys working independently and he takes his work seriously. He participates with enthusiasm in Drama and Phys Ed. He is considerate in his interaction with me. We can work together very well."

I don't think it's coincidence that I recognize many virtues in the teacher's description of Daniel's character. Children all have their own character, yet I am convinced that much of his teacher's appreciation of him is the result of his being raised with the virtues.

The Virtues Project

The Family Virtues Guide came on my path at a time when I felt stuck with raising Daniel. Linda Kavelin Popov's book so inspired me that before long I attended a course *Awakening the Gifts of Character* from the Virtues Project™. For me it was a revelation. What a positive way of raising children!

The Virtues Project sees a child as a being with all virtues - good character qualities - latent inside. Think of a sunflower seed, lying on the earth. It is destined to grow into a beautiful sunflower. But it won't get there unaided: it needs the right circumstances, the sun and moon, the earth and rain, to come to its full development.
It is not different with a child's development. For a child's virtues to develop optimally, it needs to be given the chance. The child needs its good qualities to be noticed and its less good qualities to

11

be reshaped. As parents - and teachers - you can make substantial contributions to a child's developing character.

Virtues and their language

From the Virtues Project I learned about 52 virtues and 5 simple strategies to follow in our daily interaction. My son Daniel was into his third year when we started on the virtues approach. I often encountered difficult situations as I tried to raise him where I needed to practice patience, determination and flexibility.

Linda Kavelin Popov, founder of the International Virtues Project, encourages us with the first strategy to speak 'The language of the Virtues'. When for instance your toddler is trying to tie his own shoelaces, you can say "I see you showing a lot of determination", rather than "this is taking too long, I'll do it". That certainly sounds very positive and much better for your child's self-image, but for me it was like learning a whole new language!

Recognizing teachable moments and setting boundaries

As I immersed myself into the virtues and their meaning, it becomes more natural for me to think and speak the virtues way. Daniel passed through the famed milestones of growing up: the toddler years, starting school, the beginnings of adolescence. These are the stages where children want to explore boundaries. Like many parents I tended to step in early, like in situations where something could go wrong. You want so much to protect your child, or think you know better how to go about things. Yet according to the Virtues Project, these are missed opportunities. To explore and do independently, within safe boundaries, is just what makes kids strong.

The Virtues Project teaches us to discern or 'Recognize teachable moments' in difficult situations with our children, and 'To set clear boundaries'. It is just at these points of conflict, when things go wrong, that you can both look at which virtues are needed here. That way you are stimulating qualities in your child, and not wasting important teachable moments.

Guiding the spirit

Dealing with joy and happiness usually isn't very hard to do. But what about pain, frustration, anger, disappointment and sadness? Naturally, your heart will ache when you see your child having a hard time. The Virtues Project taught me to not pass over negative feelings, but rather to listen and show interest. That way, Daniel learned that strong emotions were also a part of him, that he could openly - free of my opinions or advice - talk about. He often surprised me when I was using this fifth strategy of 'spiritual companioning' with him, by showing his sense of responsibility and his wisdom, and coming up with a far better solution to a problem or dilemma than I would have.

The way in which a child learns to deal with sadness or anger is essential for his ability to feel happy and to reflect on his own feelings and behavior.

My child can handle himself

The Virtues Project approach demands time, practice, patience and trust. For us, it has been a long-term investment. Not only has Daniel grown up to be a well-balanced person, it has also deepened our contact, and made me a steadier parent. It has brought me tranquility: 'my child can handle himself'. Time and energy: Daniel makes his own lunch, picks up his clothes and takes responsibility for his schoolwork. And above all, he looks after himself (and others!) to be happy.

The work of my heart

I have given my heart to the Virtues Project. I have integrated the virtues and the strategies in my communication training courses. This book and its real life stories of raising a child has come out of that. I hope that it will inspire you and your child(ren), and I wish you much enthusiasm and trust as you discover the virtues in your child and yourself!

Annelies Wiersma

PART 1: The Virtues in Practice

Page

How we discovered The Family Virtues Guide

"Stop it", "Hurry up", or "Let's go". We were impatient with each other when Daniel was two years old, or maybe I was impatient with him. He wanted to play one more minute with his toy cars - while I already had my coat on to bring him to the playgroup. When I finally got him to leave his cars behind, then he wanted to pick me a flower from our garden on our way out. If I wanted to lift him into his bicycle seat, he'd say: "I can do that myself." Getting him dressed: "I don't want this sweater". And so it went, the whole day long. Daniel didn't make a big deal of it if something didn't go the way he wanted it. He did go along, so I had an 'easy' child. He just invented lots of new ideas. And that made me doubt myself. I often felt guilty that I was not a fun mom because I undermined so many interesting initiatives during the course of the day. I tried to adapt to his need to discover things - we could shop for over an hour for just a few items at the supermarket. But I also spent a lot of time explaining why his plans could not be implemented: "Daniel, we are so late already, I don't have time to wait for you now." This required a lot of energy and I was exhausted by the end of the day. No time for explanations, just a sharp remark from me: "Can you for once just simply work together with me?"

I noticed that my sharp remarks hurt Daniel. He didn't do it on purpose. And he often seemed confused: what did mommy really want from him? I often felt guilty. It was uncomfortable to hear him say similar things to his friends or his cuddly toys. Children are the mirrors of their parents' behavior, painful but true.

I had not realized that raising a child was such a difficult and important task. It was pretty intensive. And how on earth do you know if you do it well?

How do you know, as a parent, that you're doing OK?

I talked to my sister about raising children and she recommended *The Family Virtues Guide*. She gave it as a present and it was the best present ever.

52 virtues are presented*, such as 'What is patience?'; 'Why would you practice patience?' and 'How do you practice patience?' It also provides you with 5 strategies** to awaken character qualities in your children and yourself. Linda Kavelin Popov assumes that everybody has all virtues, from Assertiveness to Unity. Isn't that a nice idea?

* See the list on page 187: these are all the virtues from
The Virtues Project™ Educator's Guide.

** See pages 131 and 132 (summary of the 5 strategies).

Sometimes you have to think really hard to discover the best in your - naughty - child and in yourself.

Mom, thank you for your patience

The first virtue I read in *The Family Virtues Guide* was patience. Co-incidence? I don't think so. It is a virtue we need regularly. I read that patience means that things don't always happen immediately and we sometimes have to wait. Most of our wishes don't have to be fulfilled immediately. If you think that, you will get irritated or upset if things don't happen your way, or not quickly enough. If something does not go the way you wanted it, patience can help you to remain calm and tolerant. Being patient also means that you wait if results don't happen straight away. Then it means not forcing things, but trusting in them. Being patient also includes perseverance - keep at it until it is finished, until all goals have been achieved… And, this was probably the most important insight I took from the book: you can learn patience by practicing it!

Patience is an essential quality, really. I immediately thought of lots of situations in which both of us, parent and child, could have used patience. Correction: practiced patience! We do both have this quality, but we could get better at it. That week I started paying attention to Daniel showing patience. If he was sitting quietly instead of impatiently hovering around me while I was making his drink, I praised his patience: "It's nice that you're waiting quietly while I make your drink. You show a lot of patience and so I can now make us some treats."

Initially Daniel (who was just over two years old and a late talker) would look bemused and say: "Patience, what is that?" I told him in my own words what I remembered from the description in the book. And almost every day I had the opportunity to come back to it. I kept naming it every time I saw Daniel practice patience.

At this time he was happiest playing with his toy cars. He would put them in a long line in a particular order. I was watching him do that and wondering which virtue he was showing the most: patience! I would then express my appreciation by naming the virtue: "You're showing a lot of patience (perseverance, determination…). That is a big job, but you're not stopping until it is finished." If I wanted to make a phone call without interruption I would say: "If you're patient for five minutes, I can finish making this phone call." Or after putting the phone down: "Thank you for being patient."

Daniel has all the patience in the world
while he is sorting out his cars.

It worked! Daniel was fascinated by patience. Our night time ritual included telling a story or talking about the day. Daniel now asked regularly: "Mummy, please tell me about patience." I then told him when he had shown patience that day or when I had found it difficult to be patient. He then told me when he had seen me being patient or when he himself had been patient. This bedtime chat at the end of the day also gave me the opportunity to mention his moments of patience I had not acknowledged during the day, because I still struggled with doing that. The atmosphere between us improved and became calmer. We paid attention to the good qualities of the other and we even noticed our attempts to practice patience.

Some examples of acknowledging patience:

If we found a long queue in front of the checkout at the supermarket, I would say: "This will require patience." Daniel would agree and calmness would come over us...

We can practice our patience in the long queue before the checkout.

A game in the car: "Who can be quiet the longest?" Very difficult for the both of us. So, we always ended up laughing when one of us said something first. Practicing patience became a game that we both enjoyed.

We still do. If Daniel is really enjoying the swing and I want to go home, he will say: "Mum, thank you for your patience letting me go on the swing a bit longer."

 DON'T: Don't always say "That is nice of you", or "That is really good". Children can become dependent on your compliments or they just do it to please you. If you on the other hand grumble a lot about their behavior, they will stop listening and it will make the atmosphere very unpleasant.

DO: Pay attention to the virtues your child does show and name them. Tell them how you noticed the virtue and what effect it had. When naming a virtue for the first few times, explain the meaning, use the Family Virtues Guide or the virtues cards and examples from your own lives. Give your own examples and also tell them when you find it difficult to practice that particular virtue. Children think that is funny: "That's a yummy cake, it'll be really hard to use moderation." Repeated acknowledgement and the naming of virtues your child shows will make it easier for them to identify with this 'part' of their character. You can remind them of the virtue in situations where that virtue would be really helpful but your child is not showing it. "Shall we try to be patient with your sister? She is a bit on edge because she has a difficult exam tomorrow."

Mum, please don't do that again

Once I lost my patience with Daniel (he was about four years old) when he was messing with his food. I had already warned him several times, coaxed him and ordered him to finish his plate. I was so fed up with the situation that I hit the table with my fist (much harder than planned) and said: "That's IT Daniel!" His plate with food went flying through the air. We were both shocked. Daniel said calmly, but with tears in his eyes: "Mum, please don't do that again". I promised this (and I am still ashamed when I think of it...). Nowadays if Daniel is messing with his food, I only have to say: "I am going to lose my patience very soon." We then both remember this (funny) situation and he knows what it means: "It's better to finish my food quickly!"

*Mum, would you please
not do that again?*

*I am not going to be forgiving if
Harry bashes my new bike.*

I will not forgive Harry

There are moments when I fall back into old habits of irritation, impatience and grumbling. I apologize for this to Daniel when I bring him to bed one evening. I give him a big hug and thank him in silence for his patience and tolerance; his never-ending love, even when I tell him off. I am touched every time by his compassion and forgiveness. I acknowledge this last virtue: "I am sorry for being so annoyed with you lately. Mommy should practice a lot more patience. Thank you for showing so much patience and forgiveness!"

Daniel does not know what the last word means, but he is very pleased with himself. "What does that mean?", he asks. (He will often ask what the meaning of something is). I explained that it is like giving someone a second chance. It's OK to use difficult words. They give me more opportunities to explain things: "You think it is silly what someone does, but you show understanding. You see it as a mistake and give the other person a second chance. You remember that everybody makes mistakes. You can forgive yourself and others: you give them or yourself a chance to try again. That is what you just did for me."

Although Daniel is only three years old, he understands this virtue immediately. He states with conviction: "I am not going to be forgiving if Harry bashes my new bike." I can understand that!

Daniel's response about Harry jumping on his bike shows other virtues: assertiveness and determination.

The virtue lies in the middle

We are all born with all the virtues, but there are some variations. Some virtues are developed more naturally in us than others and some virtues are developed through circumstances. I am thinking of Michael, a very patient boy. He is not likely to say in the playground: "Hey, it's my turn now!" He will patiently wait until there is "a gap" on the slide. I am not sure if he is patient by nature or - because he is chubby - has developed the "strategy" of being patient to prevent bullying. You can support Michael's development by observing him: which virtues does he show and which ones need more encouragement?

Michael shows much patience.
He could practice being more assertive.

Too much patience is not working for Michael. If he shows so much patience, he'll end up waiting forever. I feel that in Michael's case it is important he discovers assertiveness. "I have been waiting a long time, now it is my turn!" He should learn that he is as important as anyone else. Richard has clearly developed enough assertiveness. He regularly jumps the queue, using a whole range of other virtues! He knows what he wants and shows determination and purposefulness. He is very happy when sliding and clearly enjoys it. You can acknowledge all these virtues in Richard: "Boy, I can see you enjoy that slide. You're very determined to go as many times as possible. Maybe you can also give other children a go? That will show you to be considerate to other children, like Michael who also enjoys the slide. Have you noticed how long Michael has waited? He has shown a lot of patience so that you could enjoy it. Come on, Michael, it is your turn now." You can show some determination yourself when you say that last phrase. It will indicate clear boundaries to both boys.

My intervention in this case took a long time because I wanted to ensure that the children could experience the virtues - 'the teachable moment' - in this context. You could also have chosen the quicker way: "Richard, do remember that other children also want to use the slide." and "Michael, come on up. It's your turn now!"

Every day we use words such as discouraged, courage and recklessness; or careless, caring and meddling. You see how the virtue lies in the middle? You may have over-developed some virtues, while others need further development.

What I mean is that they are unbalanced and thus not working for yourself and others. Two people never have the same fingerprints and it is the same with virtues: everybody has their own unique collection. You don't have to learn them because you already have them, but you can develop them more. If you know that you're quite assertive, caring or modest, you can decide consciously to develop some other balancing virtues.

DON'T: Tell yourself 'I am impatient', 'I am not creative' and 'I don't have self discipline.' If you don't consider your-self very creative, it probably means you have little affinity with this characteristic. But you need to know you can practice all characteristics. Also don't judge others, even if you don't like their behavior ("What an untidy person you are") or just see their lack of a certain vir-tue ("Oh boy, you could use a bit more discipline!"). You devalue someone with these types of comments and are not inviting them to make some adjustments.

DO: Note which virtues someone does show in their behavior. You always show good characteristics, whatever you do. Think of a thief who shows determination and purposefulness while stealing your bike! That does not mean (s)he should disrespect the ownership of others… We have a better chance to resolve a situation if we pay attention to the best in ourselves and others.

Looking after yourself

It is nice weather and we are sitting in the garden. The rabbit hatch stands on the lawn. Daniel was given a rabbit for his fourth birthday. We bought her from the pet asylum place and found her a nice hatch. We don't know how old Lara is; she has had a lot of life experiences before we met her. We ponder this question regularly: "I think she is two" or "Do you think she could be seven already?"

Daniel likes to fantasize about this and come up with all possibilities. Suddenly Daniel notices how Lara cleans herself: "Look mom, she is washing herself." We admire how she does this. I say: "Look how carefully she cleans her feet, under her nails and behind her ears. She is really tidy with herself". I am trying to think of the virtue but find the word 'cleanliness' a bit unwieldy.

However, 'being tidy with yourself' works for me. That evening I asked Daniel to go upstairs to brush his teeth while I finish putting away the washing. Daniel is standing at the sink when I enter the bathroom. He is soaking wet, the tap is running, the sink is overflowing and the floor is a small lake. "Look mom, I am tidy with myself, just like Lara!"

Developing your own virtues language

Sometimes you discover these nice ways of expressing something that work for you. A good example is 'being tidy with yourself.' We said: "We like that one, we'll keep it!" It comes back regularly, for instance when we talk about sweets or smoking. Daniel regularly wonders: "When is something good for you?" and "When is something bad for you?". He does not want too many sweets because that is bad for you, but it is nice! Mom recognizes that. Smoking is bad, but it is nice. We acknowledge that it is good to think about this every so often and show respect for our bodies. You also look after yourself if you go to bed on time. Constantly going too late will result in ignoring the needs of your body. I suggest: "Everything that has 'too' in front is too much." Of course that is not entirely true, but we can fantasize about this endlessly: "Is five sweets too many? Is ten sweets too many?"

You see? We began with being tidy with yourself and have now ended up at moderation. This happens regularly: the next virtue follows automatically. They are like domino bricks. Touch one and many others move as well.

A whole row of virtues moves.

Using clean language

We also think about cleanliness with regard to 'using clean language'. We mean the virtue of courtesy. This is after the wee-and-poo period, which I do not mind. I do mind if children (and adults) use bad language all the time. Do 'bad' words actually exist? I don't think they do. There are people who use bad language, and some words get a bad meaning because they are used as swear words. I will not give any examples because I want to keep this book 'clean'!

Daniel and I have agreed to use as few swear words as possible and as much 'clean' language as we can. Sometimes that is really difficult, also for myself, because some words are already so 'normal'. That is my main motivation for giving the good example to Daniel: "Boy, it starts to sound normal before you know it, but it's actually not a nice word at all." This is not easy for Daniel because it is considered 'cool' amongst his friends and at school. I have asked him not to participate in this and he respects my wish. Maybe also because he understands my reasoning. We sometimes struggle, but using self discipline helps. If I fail, our game is that Daniel can correct me: "I can say a bad word too, now!" he will say with a big grin. And of course I will do the same with him.

Values, norms and virtues

You only have a small chance of success if you try to change some-one's values. However, you have a greater chance if you know which virtue is hidden beneath that value.

The virtue of courtesy or politeness often results in big discussions during my courses. One person says: "Courtesy is an old-fashioned word." "No, it isn't. That really is a virtue we should use much more," says someone else. I sometimes ask: "My dad always opens the door for me, and I like that, but who still does that nowadays?" I was in Belgium recently for work. They still know what courtesy is. It almost felt uncomfortable, but it was also nice.

Who is right? No one is and I am always pleased that this discussion happens. It becomes clear that everybody has different values and that we use these to reflect and judge. But then questions follow: "Is courtesy a value?" and "What is the difference between virtues and values?" It is fascinating to talk with others about this. Values are more person-based. One person will pay much attention to the color of the car, while another person does not care about the color as long as the engine is fine. You could say that the first person values the beauty of the car and the other the reliability of the car. Both are virtues, so both people value virtues. In fact, everybody values virtues!

Values are culture-specific, while virtues are considered important in all cultures. Worldwide, people value courage, responsibility and respect. The ways they are expressed however may differ. Leaving your shoes at the door is considered as a sign of cleanliness and respect in many Islamic countries. In the West it is considered polite to shake hands when meeting with people.

Very often people from different (sub)cultures show the same behavior. This is based on shared values. These 'group-based values' also have limits: the norms. A norm starts when you agree a limit, either verbally or silently. It is considered normal to say 'thank you' when you get a piece of cheese in the shop or to offer your seat to an elderly person in the bus...

If you don't do this, people will consider you impolite or discourteous. "If Benjamin doesn't say 'thank you' at the shop, people will look at me," says Irene. "But I do think Benjamin should say thank you without me asking for it. If I do that, it feels fake."

You should be grateful ...
But do you always have to say 'Thank you'?
Could you also do the same with a big smile?!

I think this example is more about thankfulness than politeness. I know Benjamin and his lovely smile when he is happy. I am sure he will show the shop owner his gratitude with his smile. Maybe he is still too shy to say 'thank you'. "I would not insist," I tell Irene. "It is a good idea to thank the shop owner in a friendly manner. From research we know that children copy the behavior of parents or others. So you can polish this virtue in your child by showing what are good manners according to your norm. You can invite your child to follow you in this and you show a good example yourself."

DON'T: Judge others because of their behavior or values. It gives both of you an unpleasant feeling and the other will resist immediately. This can then easily result in an argument or nasty atmosphere. There is a small chance that (s)he is willing to adapt her/his behavior or values. Don't say: "That was unreliable, unfriendly or ungrateful".... You're mis-using the language of the virtues.

DO: Value others. Look out for the intention of their behavior. Name the virtue the other shows based on her/his values. Explain which virtue you will need from the other. Reflect on: "Which boundary is being crossed for me at this moment?", "Which virtues do I value in my relationships with others?" You bring many values from the family you grew up in. Some of these values you still value. It is also possible that you appreciate others more. The main question is: "Which virtues do I want to awake in my child(ren)?"

Do you think that is courteous?

We are walking to school and wait at the zebra crossing on a busy road. A car driver stops to let us cross. "That is courteous!" I say spontaneously. I wave my hand and get a friendly nod in return. "What is courteous?" asks Daniel immediately. I explain what it means to me: you think of other people. "You show that other people are important to you and that gives a nice feeling. It makes my day if someone stops for me and that is why I thank him nicely." When searching for the right word I use some synonyms that I find easier.

Look, how courteous!

I decide that week to pay more attention to courtesy and re-read the description on the virtues reflection card. This helps me to become more aware of its deeper meaning. I am then able to explain to Daniel that courtesy is a type of friendliness with which you approach other people. It reminds me of the words of a song by the Dutch band Doe Maar: "Say please and thank you!"

I notice that I value courtesy. I am grateful to my parents for having developed this virtue in me, especially when I see how uncomfortable some adults and children are with this virtue. I am struck by realizing that all of a sudden! As a child I saw a friend struggle with using her knife and fork. 'Good manners' are a bit like tricks you can learn. But 'Not talking with your mouth full' and 'Holding the door open for someone' also mean that you pay attention to the needs of other people, treat them with respect and show that you care. Looking at it this way shows that courtesy really is an inner virtue which can be encouraged from the outside.

DON'T: Don't use the virtues to judge others. While we were practicing courtesy, we started to see the lack of it in others: "Do you think that is courteous?" asks Daniel quietly when he sees a child nearly running into an elderly lady.

DO: Pay attention to how you use the virtue yourself. It's not about what others do, but about your own behavior. Do your best. That also results in humility. There you go, another virtue. Provide others the opportunity to be courteous as well.

Looking with different eyes

The following story was told by Linda Kavelin Popov during a workshop in the Netherlands. During the break we sat in the sunshine for a cup of tea. I asked for an example of using the language of the virtues: "How do you do it and what is the effect?"

"O, there are so many examples," said Linda, while putting down her cup of tea: "I know a grandma who was weeding in her garden with the help of her grandson Jeffrey. After half an hour the little boy got bored. Grandma felt like saying: "What kind of worker are you? We have only just started and you already give up," but she kept quiet. She reminded herself what she had learned in a recent virtues workshop: find and name a virtue in the child's behavior.

Grandma thought of helpfulness. She said to her grandson Jeffrey:

"Thank you for helping me so well for half an hour. I am very grateful to you for offering your help so generously." Once started with the language of the virtues grandma enthusiastically named more qualities: helpfulness and generosity.

And by looking at it like this, she really felt it and showed that in her gratitude. Jeffrey noticed her enthusiasm and appreciation and he looked proud. Much to the amazement of his grandma, he then helped her the rest of the afternoon in the garden. Not to please her, but because he was so pleased about 'his discovery' of being helpful and generous. He discovered the joy of using these qualities."

I asked: "So because grandma - instead of criticizing her grandson - noticed one of his virtues, she stimulated him to develop this quality further?" Linda answered: "Yes, because grandma looked at him with different eyes, her grandson can now use these qualities all his life."

*To see virtues in 'naughty' children,
sometimes means looking with different eyes.*

Linda continued: "Qualities are reinforced when children get more affinity with them and use them more often. Can you see the snowball effect of this simple awareness-raising? The change in relations? The global changes possible if more people become aware of the capacities they have? If we look at what we have, not at what we don't have? Jeffrey's grandma could also have mentioned diligence or dedication."

I don't think, I talk

Daniel loves to talk. He talks a mile a minute. And so it goes during our holiday. He sits in his car seat in the back, talking about every-thing he can think of. It's impossible for my sister and myself to have a conversation. I say to Daniel: "You don't have to tell us everything you think of. Is it possible to just think instead of talk?" It is quiet for a few seconds. His memorably philosophical reply: "I don't think, I talk."

I am thinking of this one year later while we are on a bicycle ride. Daniel has met another boy at school. Four-year-old Jesse has a cleft lip and has already had many operations. He is clearly behind in language development; it is more dif-ficult to understand him than most other children in the class. The teacher has ex-plained this to the children, so they know and understand this. And she has explained how they can help Jesse. She has used a teachable moment to develop the children's compassion, understanding and helpful-ness.

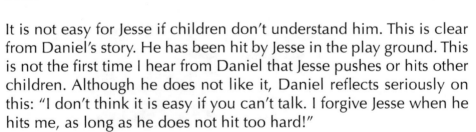

It is not easy for Jesse if children don't understand him. This is clear from Daniel's story. He has been hit by Jesse in the play ground. This is not the first time I hear from Daniel that Jesse pushes or hits other children. Although he does not like it, Daniel reflects seriously on this: "I don't think it is easy if you can't talk. I forgive Jesse when he hits me, as long as he does not hit too hard!"

I am proud of my little man, showing understanding for other chil-dren. I search for the virtue, find compassion and name this. "The virtue you show is compassion. It means that you try to understand how someone else feels." We talk a bit more about this, because as we know it isn't nice to be hit by someone: "It's OK to feel like that, you can also have compassion for yourself."

If someone gets hurt while you're playing,
you show compassion by stopping briefly
and asking: "Are you OK?"

How can we be flexible?

Daniel and I have really practiced on the virtue of flexibility. It is a virtue we all need occasionally, for instance to balance purposefulness. You will benefit immensely of these important and useful qualities if you manage to balance them in your child and yourself.

We come across these virtues without any planning on my part. I am waiting at the school at 3 PM to meet Daniel for a visit to the dentist. He and a friend come running to me: "We want to play together!" I reply: "I'm sorry but we can't; we have an appointment at the dentist." Sad faces and lots of grumbling: "But, we want to play! We already said we would."

We make a new agreement together with the children.
We do need as parents to keep our part of the bargain,
so we can show reliability.

I have to think. Which virtues are applicable here? Which virtue can I acknowledge and which one can help us? I recently read about determination and flexibility in the Family Virtues Guide, so these come to my mind: "Listen boys, I can see that you're very determined. You want to play together and had already agreed that! What a pity that we can't do that today, because we also have an appointment with the dentist. And we really can't change that. Let me think: how can we be flexible? How about if you come to play tomorrow afternoon? I was planning to take Daniel shopping for some new shoes, but we could move that to Saturday. We can all show our flexibility if we change it like this."

Could you be as flexible as an elastic band?

You know what you want

Els, the mother of Max, says during a course evening: "Max loves to play outdoors and does not want to come when I call him. "Come on Max, dinner is ready". I can call him a million times, but he won't come. We often argue about it. I find it so annoying that he won't listen to me." Els sighs: "He often does that… Max can be incredibly stubborn." These power conflicts with Max clearly demand a lot of energy from Els. She would rather eat as a family when dinner is ready and is quite happy for Max to go outside again afterwards. She is proud that he is never bored when he is outside: "Max really is an outdoor child." But the nice family atmosphere is spoiled because of Max's 'naughty' behavior. "He can forget about being allowed outside again if he does that. But I don't like that either because I know he enjoys it so much." Els clearly struggles with her own approach.

Max loves playing outdoors!

I ask Els to reflect on the virtues Max demonstrates with his behavior. She looks at the virtues poster and identifies determination. As a group we reflect on this quality: it's a beautiful quality which is very useful 'as long as it is not pushed to the extreme', as Max often does. If you do, others will regard it as being stubborn or not willing to listen. Too much determination can also be counterproductive for yourself. For instance if you're absolutely sure of something and then discover that it is wrong. It can be really hard to admit this, especially if you don't have a lot of self-confidence.

*Which virtue does Max
show in his 'naughtiness'?*

We continue with this situation. I ask her: "In which virtue could Max be stimulated?" This question is not too difficult for her. She thinks flexibility. This quality can balance Max's determination. This is a 'growth virtue', a virtue he can develop more.

I invite Els to name both qualities, determination and flexibility, in everyday situations. She can catch Max in the act of applying these. I encourage her: "Tell him. Show him what the effect is on you, on him. Explain to him in your own words what flexibility and determination mean. Thank him when he shows these qualities. Tell him when you or your husband show determination and when you're flexible. Ask him when he is determined and where or how he can be flexible."

For instance in the argument about going to bed: "Max, I know that you want to stay up longer (watch more TV…, don't want to go home…). I notice that you're very determined in that. I appreciate the way you can explain so well what you want, that's a good quality." By doing this, you give Max some appreciation and are building a bridge to more effective behavior. You can then invite him to be more flexible: "Max, it is time for bed. I am now very determined and clear. Come on, put your pajamas on. Wow, that was quick. See, you're just like an elastic band, great flexibility! We now have time for an extra long story."

You can regard this as bribery, maybe it feels like that. However, I think you show, as a parent, that you can be both determined and flexible, and the end result is: a longer story…

Virtues often work in mysterious ways

Els takes the task of naming the virtues of determination and flexibility home and reports back at the next weekly meeting: "I thought it would be very difficult to speak the language of the virtues. I'm really not used to using these words. But to my amazement Max listens to me. He understands the language of the virtues. I still find it difficult myself, but I want to practice more. The atmosphere at home is much nicer. It still has effect, even if I can't find the right word immediately. Instead of getting angry, I go quiet. And Max listens to that. He looks at me and seems amazed that he doesn't get told off. He is more cooperative and flexible, when I call him for dinner!"

*Max is flexible when he has to cut short
his marble game to have dinner.*

Virtues often work in mysterious ways. I always find it amazing to discover that children - people - show virtues, even with the most impossible behavior.

DO: Name - if necessary using the virtues list on page 187 - the virtues shown by 'naughty' children. Identify which balancing virtues could be stimulated and offer these. Tell your child that you have discovered a 'growth virtue' and that you will practice this together so that it can grow and develop. See also the exercise with the virtues balance on page 142.

My daddy knows everything!

It is great the way young children admire you while they are little. No one is as lovely as your mommy and no one as strong as your daddy! Such loyalty! When Daniel was three, he knew it for sure: "My daddy knows everything!" He would tell everyone this with conviction and pride. Some people would ask - smiling at me - "What about your mommy?" Ehmmm… he had not thought about that. A bit later he knew the answer to that question: "My mommy can do everything!" Not a bad division as parents, was it?

*Wonderful, the way your children admire you
while they are little.*

The way Daniel appreciates us as parents quickly becomes more precise: "You're the best mom in the world and you think I'm the loveliest boy. But that is logical, isn't it? Because I am your son. Tim loves his mommy most of all... I am pleased Freddy's mom is not my mommy, I don't like her..." Daniel loves to be philosophical about this: "Tim's mom is the second best mom because she is just like you. Tim is not always nice; but she will always love Tim."

This is roughly the age where you can ask a child what exactly they like, love or appreciate in other children (or adults). You can invite your child to describe this more precisely by for instance asking what the other actually does. You, or jointly at a later age, can then identify the virtues. This is a good way of learning to recognize virtues.

For example: Tim's mom is always happy and friendly. Daniel feels welcome and at home. I do know her as an hospitable and enthusiastic woman. She shows flexibility when children want to play there; they often can. In case this is not possible, she will be honest and assertive and will say so. She will sometimes negotiate: "I have no problems if they play at ours today. Can I bring Tim to you tomorrow?" Daniel also notes that: "She does not automatically defend Tim if we fight". According to Daniel this indicates that Tim's mom practices the virtue of justice.

It all feels safe to Daniel; this mom provides him with trust and reliability. Looking at the people around you gives you lots of practice to identify and recognize virtues.

Finding qualities in others is very inspiring. You will value your friends, neighbors and family differently. You will also discover more qualities in yourself. You will see how others practice certain virtues and can learn from them.

Too much virtue?

At a very early age Daniel already showed great loyalty, which I admired. I, as an adult, could really learn something from the way he made up with his friend Benjamin after a disagreement. He showed real forgiveness, compassion and mercy.

The boys have very different characters. Daniel is the 'philosopher', the talker and inventor. Benjamin is the action man. Daniel is slender and quick. Benjamin is big and strong. Daniel is careful. Benjamin is 'cool' and very physical.

Daniel does not always like the latter, but they have been best friends for many years. They often had big fights. Daniel built something with Lego and Benjamin would destroy it. I think that Daniel's endless talking and many ideas irritated Benjamin so much that he required a physical outlet. I sometimes worried that Benjamin was too physical. But the friendship with Benjamin remained strong. I often wondered: "Is Daniel showing too much loyalty towards Benjamin?" Following another fight, Daniel asked if he could go and see Benjamin. I asked him: "You're very loyal to Benjamin. Do you think you might be too loyal? What is it that you like about Benjamin? What attracts you?"

At that time Daniel was still too young to answer this. However, a year later Daniel replied: "I like it when he is there. I am less scared if Benjamin is around." Daniel clearly showed, in my view, respect for Benjamin's physical strength. "Because I have known him forever," was another answer. In the early years of primary school they really supported each other. They could not be without the other, nor be with the other. They would find each other when they needed it - I am reminded of their first school trip, so exciting for both of them. Benjamin would sometimes fight for Daniel, while Daniel would defend him verbally. Very touching indeed. Luckily by now they are a physical match and don't need to fight anymore. Benjamin has learned to explain emotions verbally instead of with his fists. They have learned a lot from each other. They allow each other their own friends. Benjamin plays soccer - he is one of the best in his team - and does judo. Daniel exchanges Pokemon cards, writes a newsletter with one friend and goes fishing with another friend. For him everything is fun as long as you can talk while doing it!

You call that a friend?

Loyalty also means being loyal, truthful and caring to yourself. Too much loyalty in a child can harm him. In the previous example I mentioned my worry about Daniel's loyalty towards Benjamin, especially when he allowed Benjamin to hit, kick, bully and taunt him. I hated that period. One day Benjamin had pushed Daniel against the slide and he had a gash in his head which was bleeding heavily. But even after that incident Daniel still wanted to play with Benjamin: "Can I go to Benjamin, mom?"

I didn't understand this and told Daniel. I noticed that I was not allowed to say anything negative about Benjamin. It took several years before he realized himself that this was not right. He mentioned being kicked by his friend (Benjamin) during a meal with other people. Andrew, a year older than Daniel, asked him: "You call that a friend? Then who is your enemy?" Daniel did laugh about this. But he started to pay more attention to his 'friendship' with Benjamin. Without mentioning this to Benjamin, Daniel became more assertive. His change in attitude made it clear that he was not accepting this physical bullying anymore. He has learned to stand up for himself while, at the same time, being loyal to Benjamin (and himself) in a healthy manner.

Using the language of the virtues to guide your children so they can stand up for themselves:

Teach a child with low self-confidence that it is OK to be assertive (stand up for themselves) when they don't like something. You can help your child by giving practical examples. For instance while play fighting say "Whoa, stop" when it becomes too rough or "I don't like this and want you to stop. I am showing assertiveness", and: "If you don't like something, you can tell me, too, and I have to listen to you."

Give a child that is hurting another child clear boundaries and say: "Stop it." Take it aside and provide clear boundaries in the language of the virtues: "We are gentle and friendly with each other. This means that we listen to each other when one of us lets us know they want this to stop."

Acknowledge the child in those moments when it shows some assertiveness: "You told Paul clearly that you didn't like it when he threw sand at you. That was being assertive."
Acknowledge the child when it stops hitting or throwing and starts listening: "I noticed you stopped throwing sand when Mary asked. You showed self-constraint and care for Mary." This way both children will gain self-confidence.

DON'T: Tell your child off when it shows - in your opinion - too much or too little of a certain quality. The child will disagree with you, defend itself or not understand you. It is not good either to talk to the other child (the bully). Correcting other people's children is not a good idea, because you're actually criticizing those parents.

DO: Pay attention to your own child. You can help them develop more self-confidence so they can stand up for themselves. Be curious. Ask your child what the reasons are for letting themselves being bullied: "What makes you accept this?", "What do you think of this?", or "How do you feel when a friend hits you?" These are open questions showing your interest without being judgmental or giving advice. Make it clear to your child that it has a choice: do I want this or not?

The development of conscience

Daniel meets Sam during the holidays. It was love at first sight. They played non-stop with each other for two weeks. One evening Daniel said: "I like Sam almost more than Tim…" This thought seemed to scare him. Was this possible? Did he not betray his best friend by saying this? It clearly was a question of conscience coming from his growing understanding of the virtue of loyalty. The Virtues Project believes that everybody has this virtue by nature. Daniel really learned this one during this holiday. The quality of loyalty was woken up when Daniel compared his innate ethical norm with a practical situation.

Daniel enjoys spending time with his new friend Sam during the holidays. But he struggles with his conscience: "Am I still loyal to my friendship with Tim?"

Our conscience allows us to make moral decisions, control 'human nature', and deciding on good or bad actions. Conscience is sometimes described metaphorically as: 'the voice of the good in human nature'. Cartoons often depict conscience as a little angel perching on your shoulder while whispering good advice in your ear.

You need an understanding of what is good and what is bad to have conscience. Young children need to develop this understanding. Parents can, according to the Virtues Project, help their children by familiarizing them with the virtues they already posses. Developing all virtues is good, but it depends on the situation which one you use at that particular moment. As a parent you support your child in learning how to focus those virtues.

My experiences show that conscience starts to form by the age of

three years. I don't consider the behavior of a child of three who kills wood lice by putting them in a glass jar as cruel. It's different when a 16-year-old kicks a dog on purpose. However, some people might never, or only partially, have developed this notion of conscience.

Your ears are smoking

One course evening we touch upon 'conscience' while talking about the virtue of honesty. "At what age can you expect this quality from a child?" asks Tamara. She mentions her son Peter and his "enormous imagination". She is wondering if she should stimulate his honesty. She wants to trust him if he tells her something, for instance about a fight between him and his younger sister. She considers trust important in their relationship. On the other hand, she also feels that the honesty should come from Peter automatically, otherwise it is just faking. As you can see, we had lots to discuss that evening.

Honesty? Your ears are smoking!!

Maria recognized Tamara's problem. Her youngest can also tell the most amazing stories. It sometimes causes confusion, but Maria recognizes most of the occasions. She will reply: "I think your ears are smoking", which to them means "you're telling tall tales". She knows she is right when Joshua starts to grin. Maria's comment lightens her son's 'lies' without being judgmental or shaming. It could easily have been those if she had said: "Josh, I can see that you're lying. You should not do that, you should be honest!" By her explanations she puts her finger exactly on what Tamara does not want to do: "I don't want to preach at my kids."

We investigate the meaning of honesty and truthfulness more by reading the virtues cards. They are very similar, but a small difference is: honesty is being truthful to others, while truthfulness is more about being honest to your self.

You can see this in the following examples: "I don't like Sophie (true feeling), but I will not tell her that (speaking honestly). I will rather tell her (white lie for the sake of tact!) that I can't play with her because I am already doing something else." Or: "You want to know who I will invite for my birthday? Well, I'll first see who invites me to theirs." (being truthful, speaking honestly).

Honesty and truthfulness - in combination with assertiveness and tact - are building stones for mutual trust. The basis of trust is that others can count on you. As with all the other virtues, trust also has an internal meaning: keeping to your own commitments.

As you can see we automatically start to talk about the virtues of assertiveness and tact because they play a role in honesty and truthfulness. We don't intend to use the virtues to preach to children. This is what the next paragraph is about.

Wagging fingers

The educational method of the Virtues Project is sometimes seen as 'wagging fingers'. And although we all sometimes do that, we don't want to be like that.

Looking at the virtues is dealing with ethical choices and moral decision making. Of course you do this from the angle of your own values and norms: what do you consider important and what agreements have you made with others. You teach your children to take a moral decision after careful consideration of all aspects. By doing this you show them their - social - responsibility. If you do it well, you're not imposing your own morality on them, from a belief you always know better, but are supporting your child in thinking through decisions and consequences.

How do you prevent yourself from nannying and mis-use of the virtues approach? A few examples will help:

You find, for the umpteenth time, a coat on the floor in the hallway. Don't say: "You should show more responsibility with your clothes." Say for example: "I saw your coat on the floor. Pity to let it get dirty like that. Will you remember to hang it on its hook? I reckon that's your responsibility. Thanks for picking it up, so your coat can look nice longer."

Your son is complaining that he forgot his Phys Ed bag. Don't say: "It is not my responsibility that you forgot your Phys Ed kit this morning?!" Say for example: "Oh, how annoying. What can help you to remind yourself of it and be responsible for taking it with you?"

It is not easy, but you can do it, especially using the exercises (see also Part 2 of this book). It is definitely worth it!

Positive and negative attention

It is very common to see children asking for attention in a 'negative' way. It is often difficult to find something good in that, but that's exactly what they yearn for. It is much more likely that their behavior will improve if we can find and acknowledge positive aspects in them.

Every child, every human being, wants to be noticed. This is a basic human need. If you don't feel loved, the next best thing is being noticed. If being admired does not work, being feared becomes the next option. This can be expressed by being annoying or 'cool' or showing aggressive behavior. The child is noticed, but in a negative way, resulting in a negative self-image. This can lead to a thinking pattern of: "See, no one loves me, likes me or thinks I'm interesting" or make them feel: "No-one even sees me." The child enters a negative circle, and growth becomes impossible.

Corrie van Dun is a special needs teacher at the Wim Monnereau school in Veendam (the Netherlands). She says: "We don't just 'look' at my school, but also 'see'. Seeing with respect means looking with the eyes of the heart. Every child has its own color. He must hear this from others and see it in their eyes. Only then will he be able to love and grow in his relationships."

I try to use a positive approach when I notice negative behavior in children that I don't like or see behavior that affects them negatively. The virtues approach is useful for me. I need to practice detachment by letting go of my own immediate opinion.

Some examples:

Tim has joined us at the swimming pool. He is moaning all the time for different things, this, that, something else. Whatever we do, it is never good enough. I ask him after a while: "Boy, you show a lot of determination today. Do you think it is possible for you to just enjoy what you have got and what we are doing this afternoon?" His answer is brief but to the point: "OK, no problem." The rest of the afternoon went fine. I am still amazed about this true story.

John is another challenge: "I want cola!", or "Why are there no sweets?", or "My dad has more computers!", or "Why do I have to take my shoes off? I don't have to do that at home!" I "have to" help him with putting on his skates. I am fed up with his behavior and say: "John, if you ask me nicely, I will be very happy to help you." He looks amazed: "Sure I can ask nicely! Please Annelies, will you help me with my skates?" I am stunned: "Of course, John, no problem. Do let me know if I do them too tightly, so we can adjust it later." And we have a pleasant afternoon afterwards.

Sure I can ask nicely!

Hey, that's not respectful!

Searching for words and learning to speak this new language - the language of the virtues - is not easy. It's even more difficult than learning Spanish or Russian. It is hard to look at others non-judgmentally or to prevent self-criticism for your own behavior. You need a lot of love, enthusiasm and determination.

But then you have those magical moments when all your efforts pay off. You just hear your child mentioning a virtue. Daniel and I went shopping one afternoon. Daniel was sitting in his bike seat behind me, chatting away as always. We "bumped" into two angry car drivers in a narrow street who were arguing frantically about a parking space. It was awful: was this adult behavior? Daniel looked at the whole situation and then commented: "Those men could use some flexibility." He had noticed which virtue was missing at that moment. It was a major confirmation for me: he "gets it", he really understands the meaning of that virtue and can apply it. He knows that you can choose to practice flexibility instead of fighting. It confirmed my efforts to master this "not-so-easy" language of the virtues.

Those men could use some flexibility.

More successes:

Erna, mother of three children, tells how her three-year-old son Tim suddenly told his six-year-old brother Jacob: "Hey, that is not respectful!", when his brother had pushed his two-year-old sister Carolien. Earlier on she had discussed the virtues card of respect with her oldest child. Erna said enthusiastically: "Tim had listened to our discussion. His comment was perfect. I was so surprised."

The teacher of group four has talked about the virtue of assertive-

hey, that's not
respectful !

ness: "You can say it clearly and nicely when someone does something you don't like." She has begun this school year with explaining the virtues of assertiveness and friendliness to avoid arguments in the playground. She hears children say to each other: "Hey, you can ask nicely if you can pass by me!" A somewhat shy child mentions his difficulty in watching the white board. His class mate notices this and says: "Miss, that was really assertive of Mark eh!"

Helen, mother of two sons, is told by her eldest son Thomas that she is foolish for being unable to lock her bike: "You're always so clumsy mom... look, this is how you do it." He shows her patiently how the lock works. At first she is annoyed because he belittles her, but - having learned yesterday about approaching her children in a positive way - she decides to let go of her irritation and find a quality in her son Thomas. "Thanks, it's great you help me so patiently. I didn't like it that you called me clumsy though. Do you really have to? Could you have helped me nicely?" Helen smiles: "Thomas looked at me and said: "Mum, you're absolutely right." I was stunned. It was such a beautiful moment! Had I moaned at him for being so rude, both of us would have become angry as we would normally have done. This approach really works!"

Could you have helped me nicely?

Daniel tells his grandma during a phone call about a great book: "You must read this book, granny. It's totally cool and has some great names in it. Those kids, boy ... they are really determined!" He notices many virtues in children's books and we often talk about it.

You should really read this, granny. It is totally cool.
Those kids, boy… they are really determined!

What about emotions?

In the previous story Helen was really helped by detaching herself from her anger and choosing a positive approach while searching for a quality in the behavior of her son Thomas. I can turn my irritation about Daniel, Tim or John into the search for and acknowledgement of a virtue in these children. It provides clarity and better contact if we express clearly what we need. Humans - both children and adults - are not always aware about the effect of their behavior on others. Naming this behavior can provide clarity and improve relationships.

Course participants will immediately ask: "Does that mean that I am not allowed to show my feelings?" They consider this highly unrealistic. "You should be allowed to be angry with your children every so often. They will learn from that. If you can't show your feelings, you will be walking on eggs all the time and that is not natural. It is not healthy to hide your feelings." Or: "If I am angry, the children will understand straight away that they have gone too far."

Emotions are certainly allowed. They alert you that a virtue is missing. Try to recognize the teaching moment and provide the missing virtue.

An example:

Your daughter drops her clothes all over the place; you're disappointed and feel like a drudge... Maybe you think you have failed in your efforts to raise her... Your child is crossing your boundary... You have already shown tolerance several times... She is still not listening, so you get angry... You wonder if she will ever listen to you... What will become of her?

Maybe I am exaggerating a bit, but emotions can boil over easily. As parents of our children we expect them to do well. Children by nature will want to do the right thing as well. That is why it is so important to teach them what you do appreciate. Don't burden them with your anger, accusations or negative comments. This will cause much frustration and confusion for both of you. Anger often only provides satisfaction for a very short period of time.

It is more effective - and much more pleasant for all concerned - to detach yourself, count to ten and reflect. What is happening? What is causing this emotion? What affects me so much? What do I need? What do I need from the other? If you then communicate in the language of the virtues, you can often solve it quite easily: "Milly, I notice all your clothes in your room. Yesterday I asked you to put the clean clothes in your wardrobe and the dirty ones in the wash. I am sorry that I can't wash them for you now. What can help you to keep our agreement and treat your things with care?"

What can help you to care for your things?

Spanking is educational?

Dad Ruben is sure: "It works best if I spank Benjamin. He asks for it if he continuously does not listen to me. He will scream but it also works." Ruben looks at me triumphant. I can see him thinking: "Well, what do you say to that? I am right, aren't I?"

Dad Ruben does not accept
Benjamin's disobedience.

Little Benjamin is only two years old. His dad has told him several times that he is not allowed to open the door of the oven. Benjamin enjoys opening and letting it fall shut again. He does not hear what his dad says because his unconscious mind leaves out the word not. What he hears is: 'Play with the door of the oven' and he likes that because it's a great game. That is, until his dad gets angry and boxes him around the ears. He is shocked and cries. He immediately stops playing with the oven door and climbs on his dad's lap to seek comfort.

*Little Benjamin enjoys opening
and closing the door of the oven.*

Dad Ruben thinks his approach works, but is that true? I ask Ruben what happened to him that he got so angry. He comments that it irritates him when his son does not listen: "Children must be obedient, otherwise there will be chaos." I ask Ruben what he was trying to teach his son at that moment. He is quiet for a while. "I want to teach him that the oven is hot and that he should stay away from it. Secondly I think he should show respect if something is not allowed. He must leave some things alone because they are not his. Children should not touch everything." I ask Ruben if he can explain this the next time to Benjamin in this way. Ruben thinks he can do that, it is after all logical and clear. I ask him which virtue can help him. He finds perseverance. Other course participants confirm that children sometimes need to hear things several times before they sink in. This requires some investment, perseverance and trust, for instance to teach a child to treat possessions of others with respect. This is the virtue alternative for "don't touch".

Teaching children self-restraint is important in situations where they would like to pick up or touch something while this is not allowed. You can practice this with your child: "Just look at all the nice things in this shop! Shall we choose something together to watch very carefully? Which one is the most beautiful, you think? Maybe we can touch that very carefully with just one finger? Wow, you can do that very carefully! So it stays nice and whole. It takes self-control from us, doesn't it?"
I just want to remark that many people get really annoyed with "children who touch everything". In these instances you could say: "All the things in this shop are of that lady. She probably wouldn't like it if we touch everything. Let's respect her wish; also we won't break anything like that."

You will be using a whole range of virtues yourself while supporting your child during its teachable moments. As parent I realized that detachment, self-discipline and responsibility helped me to recognize and use a teachable moment: detachment in leaving behind my anger, irritation or other emotions; self-discipline to take the time to reflect on the question: "What can we learn from this?"; responsibility to take my role as parent serious and ask myself: "What can I teach Daniel in this situation?". This three-step-method didn't feel 'natural' in the beginning, but together with Daniel I encountered many lovely teachable moments, opportunities to recognize and develop our virtues.

Out of his anger - and concern that Benjamin would hurt himself - Ruben used his physical power on his son. The effect of this educational method is that children obey out of fear. When they get older, they tend to strongly oppose their 'authoritarian' father or mother. In these kinds of circumstances children don't learn how to develop their qualities. They don't hear what IS expected of them and don't learn from the situation, the teachable moment.

DO: Recognize teachable moments. Identify, using the virtues list if necessary (on page 187), which virtues your child can develop. Find out which virtues can be stimulated and offer these after - if possible - you have acknowledged the virtues your child has shown. Also identify which virtue can help you during a teachable moment. Regard it as a joint challenge to develop your virtues.

Growing in an environment of trust

I often get asked what I think of punishment and reward. Can you raise children and set boundaries without punishment and reward? Yes, you can. I rarely use reward or punishment since I have started using the virtues approach. If I ever happen to use either of them, it feels like I am manipulating the situation.

Many people agree that punishment is damaging, but it might be new to them that rewarding can have the same effect. But that is the way it is.

As a parent you want your child to become independent and know how to react adequately in different situations. Whether a child feels content about it-self should not depend on your opinion. The virtues approach acknowledges the important role of parents to support the development of their child's own, in-ner authority. It therefore does not help to punish the child for not finishing its plate (authoritarian parent) or to negotiate and praise when it does finish its plate (democratic parent). The combination of negotiation followed by giving in or becoming angry is extremely confusing for all involved.

The second part of this book, from page 129 onwards describes different educational styles. You can use it to become aware which style you use to set boundaries for your child.

Having a nice family meal together

"What is the best way to react at the family table, when one child messes around with his food? Or if a teenager is always home late? Or if all children talk at the same time and they don't listen to the others or their parents?" It is Maria who asks these questions one evening. They are very recognizable 'problems' for all parents. It is difficult to react in the right way, especially if you're already 'in the middle of it'.

The key question is: what would you like to happen during meals? What is important to you? What do you value most? What do you value less? I normally give the parents a bit of time to reflect on this. Each will discover, individually, what is most important to them: eating healthy is important for your body and your energy levels; leaving food on your plate is a waste of money or unfair to other children who do have to eat; having a meal together should be a nice experience, a period of calmness in the family... The art is then to find ways for you to create the circumstances which will allow your values to be respected. You could choose a number of virtues as starting points to give you a guideline. You can read more about this from page 155 onwards.

Examples:

Cooperation: we pay attention to each others needs. We take the time to eat together. We expect everybody at the table at 6 PM so we can eat together.

Respect: we take a small amount of food at the time. We will finish what is on our plate. This is our way of showing respect to the earth and the food it produces.

Self-discipline: we listen to each other and wait until the other has finished talking. NB: You could also choose 'justice' as your starting point: taking turns to speak is fair.

Clear agreements prevent family meals becoming frustrating occasions. Everybody knows what to expect and confirms the mutual agreements. This is sometimes easier said than done. "How do you maintain consistency?" asks Maria. You can remind each other of the agreements by mentioning: "Don't forget the others."

Of course you can pay attention to circumstances, for instance: once a week you're allowed to leave something on your plate if you really don't want it.
Because it is your experience that this happens about once a week, it can be done with respect in this way.

You can also jointly come up with consequences of making up the situation. For instance: if you're late for the evening meal, you will have to set the table the next day. Children will learn how to make choices and will develop a sense of responsibility while thinking about how to correct a situation. They will often do this joyfully, without punishment or reward. You can read more about the use of and agreeing on consequences from page 157 onwards. Finally you can think of some virtues that can help you to be consistent: determination or - occasionally - flexibility.

We now stand for something!

Monica was a participant in one of my first courses. This is what she told me a year later: "My family and I are now more positive with greater vitality. We're radiating something now. I was raised as a child with a strong emphasis on virtues such as cleanliness and politeness. As a mom I chose a looser, democratic approach. I gave my daughter and two sons more space and gave them lots of space to voice their opinion. I learned during the virtues course that this approach could have a confusing effect, with my children's freedom of expression sometimes bordering on rudeness. I recognized the need for more boundaries and sticking to them.

So I sat down with my husband and the children. Jointly we drew up a poster with house rules, such as: every morning you have fifteen minutes to wash, brush your teeth and comb your hair. Every day we would pay attention to our good intentions. And you know what? It worked! My husband and children are becoming more and more involved and enjoy participating. We have developed a 'loose tidiness'. Our family now stands for something," she concludes happily.

Boundaries, based on virtues, help parents by providing an appropriate structure for their children without using force. Boundaries invite children as well as educators to bring out the best in themselves.

Listening without rescuing

Daniel 'suddenly' does not want to go to Sophie's birthday party. How annoying, I am thinking. We only just bought a nice present. A bit hard on Sophie. You can't do that! I decide to be curious instead of voicing my feelings and opinion. I use the seven steps of spiritual companioning* to discover what is happening:

Daniel: "I don't think I want to go to Sophie's party. I don't feel like going."
… … … … …
Me: "You're wondering if you want to go because you're not sure it will be a nice party?"
Daniel: "Yes, I don't know yet. Hmm, I really don't feel like going."

"Tell me, what is the matter that you don't feel like going to Sophie's party?"

---

* See pages 165+ and the scheme of the process on page 188

Me: "What is the matter? What is the most difficult?"

… … … … …

Daniel: "I don't know Sophie that well and I have never been at her house. I don't know her parents and I might not like the cake."

Me: "You don't like going because you don't know Sophie's parents and are worried that you might not like the cake but have to eat it?"

… … … … …

Daniel: "Well, I don't think I have to eat the cake. Sophie's parents are not that mean. And it is only a birthday party… Sophie has also been to my birthday party…"

Me: "So maybe the cake is not the problem. You know Sophie's parents a little. You think you should go because Sophie has also been to your party. But you're worried that you might not like it. What can help you to worry less, you think?"

… … … … …

Daniel: "… Maybe I can call you if I would like to leave earlier?"

Me: "That is fine, if that makes you feel better. How will you organize that?"

Daniel: "I will then ask Sophie's mom if I can call you because I would like to go home earlier."

Me: "That sounds like a good plan. I am sure it will work. I am glad you have been so open and honest in talking with me. What has been helpful in talking about it?"

Daniel: "It does not look so scary now. It would not have been nice for Sophie if I had not gone to her party. She has also been to mine and I would be sad if children didn't want to come if it was my party. But calling you is a good solution and I am happy with that. It means I can come home if I don't like it."

I finish our 'round' of companioning by saying: "I can see that you also trust that it will be fine and it will be a nice party. It is courageous of you to go, even though it is a bit scary. I am pleased you care about Sophie's feelings and that she can count on you at her party!"

I am pleased that I have acknowledged Daniel's feelings and have offered him companioning in this situation. I was curious instead of angry or disappointed. Listening to Daniel helped him to express his feelings and he made the moral decision. Had I said something like "You can't do that", he would have become defensive and we would have been arguing over it. This time he was able to investigate for himself what was going on, because I took him seriously, and he found the answer himself. I supported him in this teachable moment by using spiritual companioning and acknowledging him for his virtues: being caring, showing compassion and courage.

DON'T: If your child feels strongly about something, it's better to hold off a bit with your opinion. Don't immediately offer a solution. Don't advise. Don't ask closed questions: "Don't you want to go to the party?" Your 'rescuing' will have the opposite effect and your child will close up. Maybe he'll even get angry with you and say: "You don't understand!"

DO: Offer companioning if your child has strong feelings about something - when it is anxious, sad or angry, or if it has a dilemma. You will help your child to make a place for its emotions. Listen with your full attention. Ask questions that will help to unburden and which get to the heart of the matter: "What did you feel then?" or "What is the most difficult in this situation?" and "What could help you?" Also ask what has become clearer and acknowledge those beautiful qualities your child shows during that teachable moment.

You're responsible when we're biking together

We are driving to a friend of Daniel for a play date. We have known Abe for many years. He used to live close to us, but they moved to a village in another province a few years ago. Far away, but not forgotten. Due to the distance they don't see each other often, but when they do they will play together like they always did. They are still 'best friends'. That's a true friendship.

This road to Eext is a dangerous dual carriageway. You're allowed seventy miles per hour, but overtaking is forbidden. There have been so many deadly accidents that the road is called 'the death road'. Suddenly another car zooms past, scaring me to death, and requiring me to brake hard to let him get in front of me to avoid an accident. "How irresponsible!" I shout angrily.

I am scared to death
when I am suddenly overtaken.

"What do you mean, mom?" asks Daniel. I explain about the risks taken by that driver, not just for himself but also towards other road users such as us. The rule on this road is that you don't overtake and I consider it very unwise if people still do that. There are many road signs to remind you of the rule. We read them together: 'Speeding is for dopes', 'You won't get home any quicker in an ambulance'. These sort of signs are to remind people of their responsibility. "But," I point out to Daniel, "being responsible is something you do automatically, that feels good to you from the inside because you don't want to endanger yourself or others."

We talk more about responsibility. Daniel knows exactly when I am responsible: "You're responsible for me when we bike to school together. I must always bike very close to you, on the inside." That is true. "Heel doggie!" I will say jokingly. We laugh about that.

I tell him I see him acting responsibly when he turns off the TV because there is something scary on it and he does not think that his younger friend should see that. "You also show that you care," I say, naming another virtue.

"I am responsible for the cat," says Daniel. "She didn't know the area when we just got her. So I always made sure that the garden gate was closed, so that she could not escape or get lost." It is good to chat about responsibility, time flies and before we know it we arrive at Eext.

Loads of confidence

We regularly discuss responsibility that week. This has always been the case with all virtues. Somehow Daniel is fascinated by them, just like other "adult" expressions such as "taking risks".

It makes my life easier, for instance when I see his bike left outside: "Daniel, will you put your bike in the garage please? If you leave it outside it might get rusty or even get stolen. I usually pay attention that you don't leave your bike outside, but I think you can be responsible for it yourself from now on." And on a day he forgot about it: "Remember to be responsible for your bike?" Or if he wants to build something with his friend: "Yes, you can borrow my tools as long as you're responsible for their safe return."

I enjoy seeing Daniel's sense of responsibility grow. I can let him do things on his own while he is still small. Over time he walks home by himself from school, stays alone at home for a short while or goes to the supermarket, full of confidence, for some shopping. Step by step we broaden his responsibility and his boundaries (in the sense of his freedom). The latter explicitly: in what area is he allowed to play? We agree that he will tell me where or with whom he is going to be. If I can trust him to keep important agreements, I know I don't have to worry. This way Daniel develops his responsibility, trustworthiness and confidence.

Showing character

A quote from Dr. Dan Popov: *"The individual virtues are powers that come from deep inside, from the kingdom of virtues!"*

What you want to see as a parent is for your child is to have a 'good' or 'strong' character, to know he or she is honest and just, and that your child shows 'character' if called upon.

I have noticed that when I think of the meaning of the word character, I think of virtues. Virtues turn out to be essential for our character, they are the core. Someone's inner strength is based on virtues.

Purposefulness, determination and perseverance are virtues that provide the inner strength to do the right thing. Love, justice and tolerance support your moral decision-making. Virtues are found in everyone, young and old. However, not in obvious behavior - the outside - but more at a deeper level. They are the intention, they inspire positive behavior. They always let one's inner strength shine out. I often remind myself that everybody often acts from an inner sense of what feels like the right thing to do.

You could ask: "But what is the right thing?" That of course varies in every situation, from time to time, and day by day. Whatever the moment demands determines the right virtue. When you try to do the right thing, virtues are always a part of it. If you want to discover what the right thing is in a situation, ask yourself which virtue you need to deal with it. Virtues are like mirrors. They reflect, showing you how to be 'good' and live according to the highest values. They are the foundation of every moral decision. The beauty is that once you have made such a decision, you will always find supporting virtues to lead you and help you in your acts.

Looking out for number one does not create character. Neither does copying what others do, or doing something just because it is easier, safer or more acceptable. However, if you do something based on virtues, such as love, loyalty or justice, your motive is pure, whether it's you or someone else that benefits. You can be sure you're doing the right thing when your actions are based on virtues.

Doing the right thing can require courage, purposefulness, determination, tolerance or other virtues. It is not a question of 'timing' but more of necessity, although wisdom - another virtue! - plays an important role in determining the right moment.

If you ask real heroes why they did it, they will tell you: "I just had to do it" or "Someone had to act."

In certain situations you will act immediately because your inner self tells you to.

The most important role of parents

Every parent plays an important role in the development of his or her child. The virtues, keys to our character, are latent in every child, right from the beginning.

In every bulb or seed, you will find the whole plant. It is the same with people. Every human being has character qualities, the virtues. If you look after them, they can become capacities and skills. If you don't look after them, they will stay dormant. If you develop them incorrectly, they will get all tangled up and lead to confusion.

*In order to grow and flourish
we need a good soil,
light and love.*

Everybody has all the virtues, but individual differences exist in the level of specific virtues. Some people have lots of patience by nature, others don't. Everyone - you, your child, your parents, your brother, your sister, your grandparents - has a different mix. If you develop yours, you will get the character that suits you. And what is so great and encouraging is that it is never too late for further development

Are you not naturally tidy?
It's never too late to adjust your character
and awaken some virtues…

Your behavior at any moment is determined by your particular mix of virtues, and how well-developed these are. Your character is not based on age, but on development.

You will have the inner strength to use a specific virtue demanded by a situation if you have practiced and developed it enough. If you have not done this, you will be lacking. Your character keeps developing. We do not know our own capacity until a virtue is really tested: when we have reached the end of our patience, or have become discouraged.

As a parent you can stimulate character development by naming and acknowledging every latent virtue which has found some expression, in such a way that the child notices this and accepts it. Character consolidates when children develop their affinity with virtues and practice them more consciously. Character qualities - virtues - are not abstract. They can be understood as behavior that is inspired from the inside. No one has to fail. Each time a virtue is required that has not yet been well-developed, it's a wonderful teachable moment. As a parent you can help your child to successfully practice and develop a virtue.

It's not nice to trick small children

Let me give you an example to show you what it means to use virtues for moral decision making.

Daniel meets his neighbor Kim in the street. Kim has just been given a pack of Pokemon cards. At that time, these are 'way cool', and much trading goes on at home and at school. Daniel can't wait to see Kim's new cards. Who knows, there might be some cards which he can use to complete a set. That's interesting! But Daniel will need to be patient because we go to taekwondo lesson first. In the dressing chambers Daniel tells another friend, with much excitement, what he is going to do when he gets home. Nathan asks in a slightly preachy tone: "How old is your neighbor? I don't think it is fair to trick younger children in giving up their expensive cards. They don't know the real 'value' of those. I don't think that's fair at all."

Is it fair to exchange Pokemon cards with children who don't know much yet?

I am curious how Daniel will react. I was of a similar mind as Nathan but had not said anything yet.

Daniel looks slightly disappointed. You can almost hear him think: "Is Nathan correct or is it different for me?" I know he is thinking the latter when he says: "I remember when I was small; I would exchange cards with older children. I'd get many in return for a single card and was very pleased with that. I didn't yet understand the value of a specific card. So I do think it is fair to ask Kim to exchange his cards."

Looking at it like that makes fairness very relative. Daniel made a moral decision. He searched for a way to act fairly in this trading deal. He took responsibility for his decision. Neither Nathan - nor I - had anything to add to that.

The good Samaritan

A Jewish man traveled from Jerusalem to Jericho. He was robbed by highwaymen. They took all his clothes, beat him nearly to death and left him lying on the edge of the road. A priest passed, but when he saw the man, he crossed to the other side of the road and ignored him. A passing temple official acted in the same way. Luckily for the man a third person passed by who did have compassion. This person was a Samaritan. The Samaritan knelt next to the man, cleaned his wounds with oil and wine, and covered them with cloth. He then lifted him on his donkey and walked next to it*.

In this story two well-respected people - a priest and a temple official - didn't want to be bothered helping the victim of a violent crime, while the Samaritan was helpful. And we know that the Jews looked down on Samaritans at that time. But what is important is not who someone is, but what he or she does.

One day Daniel, seven-years-old, discovers mercy. He is going to the supermarket for some shopping. A homeless man is standing at the entrance. Daniel chats to the man and buys the Big Issue (the homeless people's magazine). When he gets home, he tells me the whole story: "That man at the supermarket is from Bulgaria. He sells the Big Issue because he is saving for a bike.

* The parable of the Good Samaritan comes from the Bible.

When he has saved enough money, he will cycle all the way to Bulgaria. I have given him two euros and hope he will succeed."

I have to laugh to myself. Two euros, why not, it's my money after all. But I am also pleased that my son showed an interest in the well-being of a homeless man. And that he was interested enough to want to give a hand (or euros in this case) to that man's dream to return to his home country once he had earned enough money.

I say to Daniel: "You really did show mercy!" Another virtue named and explained to Daniel. I could also have used the qualities of compassion or charity. In this context all of these virtues have roughly the same meaning, but I preferred to use an 'old-fashioned' word this time.

Letting go

Raising children is also letting go. At the age of three, Daniel is allowed to cycle in the alley and on the square with the playground. He practices responsibility and reliability. I practice detachment (letting go). We both increase our (self-) confidence.

We both practice virtues
when Daniel cycles in the corridor.

Every so often we consult, as circumstances change, about whether Daniel is up for a new responsibility or if we should wait a bit longer because it is too soon. I recently asked Daniel if he wanted to go to the swimming pool with Harry. I didn't feel it was necessary anymore to accompany them, but the boys were not so sure yet. At other times I am the one feeling it's too soon. In those moments I show my appreciation for Daniel's self-confidence but ask him to respect my - temporary - hesitation.

We have built a respectful relationship based on virtues. A relationship where we don't have to fight. Daniel can develop in freedom within safe boundaries. I trust him.

DON'T: Expect certain behavior from your child too early. For instance: "You're not allowed to take sweets." It is normal for young children to only be obedient when you are present. Prevent disappointment and failure. Don't ask children to show a virtue which is still outside their ability.

DO: Make it clear to your child what is allowed and where the boundary is. Make sure you take the age of the child and your own feelings into account. Is your child ready for this new hurdle? Are you ready? Which virtues can guide you both?

Time out

We heard the term 'peace zone' from a neighbor. When we've been out together, to a playground or the beach, and after we have had enough of that, we all go into our 'peace zone'. This means everybody goes back to their own home for a snack, a bath or the like. We like this idea because you always feel better after peace zone.

Daniel is watching a television program when the doorbell rings. It is Harry asking if Daniel wants to come and play. Daniel hesitates and then says: "No, not at this moment, I am having my peace zone. Come back in an hour or tomorrow afternoon. I would like to play with you then." Harry has no problem with that. The boys say goodbye and Daniel goes back to his chair. Within seconds he is watching his cartoon again.

I am in my peace zone.

I admire the way my son indicated clear boundaries in a friendly and tactful manner without offending Harry. Daniel showed integrity and self discipline because he thought about his own needs before replying to Harry. I can learn from this because I often struggle with unexpected visitors. I will invite him or her in, even though I might not have the time. And even when they ask: "Is this convenient?" I will reply nine out of ten times: "Yes, of course…"

Phone calls are the same: "Have you got time to talk?" I find it very difficult to reply with a nice and firm no . Sometimes my parents call, just when I am hitting my stride with writing: "I just wanted to hear my daughter's voice. How are you and the family?" I have learned from Daniel to say: "I really appreciate that you're interested and I would love to talk to you some other time. Will you be in tonight? I am writing an article which needs finishing and the words are just flowing nicely." My dad replies: "No problem, let's talk tonight and you can tell me all about it. Talk to you later!"

Childhood baggage

A while ago, Albert, Harry's dad, came to pick him up and kept chatting. I asked him and his son if they could hurry up a bit because I was trying to meet a deadline. Albert apologized, and they left. Later on I was wondering if I had handled this situation well. Had I been too direct? I often feel I'm not tactful enough.

Maybe that comes from my childhood? We owned a shop and we learned to always be ready to be of service to others. Someone entering the shop after closing time, saying: "I just remembered my neighbor's birthday. Can I still buy flowers please?" No problem, the customer is king, even if we had all just sat down for dinner. We learned to make good notes if someone phoned for dad while he away. My partner just tells the caller that I am not at home: "Well, they can call again, can't they?"
With my customer-centered attitude from my childhood I just think: 'Yes, but you could also have offered that I will call them back'.

Can I help you?

My parents are still like that: ready to be of service to everybody. They are the most flexible, accommodating, hospitable and helpful people I know. These are qualities I admire in them, but that can also annoy me . I get irritated if someone calls me late in the evening about my work: "What is this person thinking? What makes them think they can ask me about work this late?" But I will always answer in a 'customer-friendly' manner. This is different from 'friendly' because I don't feel like that at that moment. I sometimes let Daniel answer the phone if I don't feel like it. He will say without any problem: "My mommy is reading me a story and has no time to come to the phone, sorry. Bye-bye!" I feel naughty then. I am impressed by Daniel's skill of being assertive in a friendly way. I am often too shy to do the same, but keep telling myself to follow his example.

~~~~~~

DO: What - which qualities - did you bring from your childhood? What about that do you value? When do you feel it is not working for you and that it is better to use another quality? Another eye opener could be: Which virtues have you learned from your children?

DON'T: Still blame your parents when you're eighty!

~~~~~~

In love!

Daniel and I are at home alone one evening. Snuggling up on the couch after dinner, we philosophize on life. We talk about being in love. This greatly occupies Daniel because he very much likes a girl in his class. I have heard many stories about her. "She reminds me of you mom, she is smart and nice," says Daniel. I am honored!

There is one problem however. His friend Joshua is also in love with her. Joshua is a nice boy, the smallest of the class. He is very cuddly and has a lovely smile with which he charms everybody. Gina likes both boys. As she would, with all that attention!

A confident Daniel tells me: "Gina thinks I'm clever, we work well together and I often make her laugh. We also talk a lot."

Being in love requires many virtues.
After all, you want to show your best side.
It also makes you vulnerable.

I am glad that Daniel shares his feelings so openly with me and acknowledge this. He comments that he is not that open to everybody because you can also get teased about it. I comment: "Your honesty has made you vulnerable as well". Daniel recognizes this. I promise not to tease him with his love because I don't want to hurt him. I would rather enjoy his butterflies together.

This is not the first time we have talked about teasing and being hurt. We know that people can say hurtful things to each other. We know you can prevent this putting yourself in the other's shoes and try to be thoughtful. Tactfulness can help you to convey a difficult message in a way that does not hurt.

Vulnerability is also a beautiful virtue. Sometimes it is confused with weakness which I think is a pity. I personally think it shows strength when someone is able to show their vulnerability. People who dare often have a lot of confidence, otherwise they would not show this virtue spontaneously.

However, as with other virtues, it is important not to 'overdo' vulnerability because you can easily get hurt. Balance can be provided by some reservedness. The ones who act as if nothing can touch them may be regarded as staunch, but also as rigid and closed-off. They never allow themselves to express their real feelings or share them with others, and never can ask for help.

Do you want to see her grave?

One afternoon Daniel uses the three traumas in his life to impress Gina: his scar (bitten by a dog when he was two); his dead rabbit (buried in our garden: "Do you want to see her grave?") and his parents (divorced six years ago). Ha, Joshua can't beat that! Very creative.

The boys sometimes nearly fight to get Gina's attention. Their friendship started to suffer under the strain of joint attention for this cute girl. Daniel tells me how irritating Joshua is. At school they sit at the same table with Gina and one other girl. Daniel says: "Joshua always wants compliments from her for a painting he has made or an exercise he is doing. It is driving me nuts."

I think back of my own childhood. I tell Daniel that when I was six years old, two boys, Kieran and Mark, were in love with me. They also were best friends. They both wanted to marry me and did everything they could to be chosen by me. I wonder what happened to them. They both lived at a farm and I often played with them. Not at the same time, though, that would have resulted in a fight.

Daniel can imagine how Kieran and Mark felt. He asks tactfully: "What was it like for Kieran that Mark wanted you as well?" I have to confess that I have no idea. I wasn't thinking about that at all at the time. Daniel asks: "But who did you love?" I have to think hard: "Sometimes Mark and sometimes Kieran. I definitely didn't like it when they fought because of me."

Daniel has to think about this. I can see in his face that he is taking my little tip on board. I do hope my tactic works, both for the friendship between the boys as well as for Daniel. Of course, I secretly hope that Gina will find 'my' Daniel the nicest and will come visit the rabbit's grave.

And so it happens. With a little help from me they have a nice afternoon together. The chat we had has also helped the relationship between Daniel and Joshua. They regularly meet again to play. Their friendship seems - for the moment - to be restored.

A fight is resolved while fishing.
Extraordinary how quickly children can detach themselves
and forgive each other.

Smelly voice

We talk again about being in love. Daniel tells me that Jonathan is also in love. "Not with Gina?", I hope. Curious now, I ask: "So who is he in love with?" Daniel answers he can't tell me because he promised Jonathan. I spontaneously praise him for his integrity, the virtue he just showed so firmly: "Of course you shouldn't tell me. That way, you show you have integrity."

"What is that?" asks Daniel. I explain in simple terms: "Sometimes you want to tell something that is a secret. It's exciting to pass on a bit of news, or sometimes it's difficult to keep a secret because it's so surprising. But if you keep your promise not to tell, you show the other person your integrity.
It is also a kind of reliability. The other's secret is safe with you. I am sure your friend Jonathan appreciates that. He made himself vulnerable by telling you his secret, because what would happen if you would tell others?"
Daniel answers immediately: "Jonathan would not tell me another secret any time soon, because I made him look silly." I reply: "Exactly, that is why it is so nice to see your integrity. It is important in building strong friendships. We could not feel safe with another if integrity is lacking."

We automatically end up talking about gossiping, another new word which I need to explain to Daniel. I explain: "Gossiping is saying nasty things about people who are not there." Daniel recognizes this: "Sometimes we say that John's voice smells, or that Tim has no nice toys." I ask him: "Do you know why we sometimes gossip?"

That's a difficult question for Daniel. He is right, it is a hard one. We brainstorm together. Is it our enthusiasm? Do we hope that the other person shares our opinion so that we are not the only one? Or are we consciously trying to exclude someone we don't like?

How do you tell someone tactfully
that his voice smells?

It is unfair, really: the one being talked about can't defend himself. How come we are so mean sometimes? Is it revenge because others are sometimes mean towards us? What's the effect of gossiping on friendships? We can't find an answer. But we do discover that we would not like it if other people gossiped about us. And that we should stop and think before joining in: "You can choose not to do something, even if it is very attractive. That requires self-discipline. You can tactfully start talking about something else when others are gossiping. Or you can say it is not a nice thing to say about that person."

It is also useful for me to reflect on this. We mention a few more examples - teachable moments- for both of us. Our talk has reminded us of various virtues.

Biting your tongue

A standard question to during the Virtues Project parenting course is: "What are the strong character qualities in your child?" These are qualities that require no extra effort and manifest themselves from a very young age. We often ignore these qualities as parents because we don't need to stimulate these. We almost automatically assume our child has that particular quality. Maybe because we ourselves have that quality and think it is normal?

Both Daniel and I have a lot of enthusiasm. We get enthusiastic about things very easily. We take a lot of initiative. We are optimistic and look on the bright side of things. It's a good quality which helps us to get things done. Our enthusiasm is contagious. And our enthusiasm helps us to try again if something goes wrong.

By reflecting on this, we value and appreciate this quality more and become more effective in its use. Sometimes a quality is so strongly developed that it requires a balancing quality. If your child is too honest, you, as a parent, could help it to develop more tactfulness. This will enable your child to use its honesty more effectively. Too much honesty ("That is an awful dress") is often not effective. When Daniel and I are too enthusiastic, this can actually deter others. They feel we are overpowering and don't give them space. For us, it can be quite a challenge to control ourselves and show some restraint.

A group of children from the neighborhood plays outside regularly. They play hide and seek, bike or play with marbles. Young and old play together. Ten-year-old Harry introduces a new ball game one afternoon. He tries to explain the rules to everybody. Easier said than done. How was it again? Benjamin becomes impatient, he isn't getting it at all. This prompts Daniel - seven years old - to take over from Harry. He already figured out how to play this new game!

I imagine that's about how it went after Daniel gets home disappointed. He does not want to join in again; they think he is a know-it-all. He explains what happened. I show him that I understand by paraphrasing his story. I acknowledge several virtues he has shown - even in this difficult situation. "You were enthusiastic about the game and wanted to help by explaining the rules so that you could start quickly. But it didn't happen like that and now you don't want to join in anymore." Daniel perks up with my acknowledgement of his enthusiasm and helpfulness. But my last comment, that he does not want to join in anymore, makes him sad.

Daniel feels responsible for explaining the game

Coincidentally, I had a similar experience last week. Perhaps not such a coincidence, after all we share that enthusiasm. I also recognize the resistance it can create in others if I push my ideas on them. I decide to tell Daniel about my experience.

I was chairing a meeting where everyone was invited to share new ideas. I suddenly got a bright idea, explained this and went straight into sorting out the details. Being so enthusiastic about my new idea, I completely forgot to listen to others and didn't allow room for their ideas. That is, until one of the participants corrected me. She told me that this was not brainstorming and that she felt as if the decision had already been taken. She was right of course. I had been steamrollering everybody in that meeting!

"Of course I didn't mean to do that," I told Daniel, "Even so, others can experience it as domineering. I didn't mean to and I also know that you don't want to do that. What I have learned is that sometimes it is better to just listen to others. Instead of always taking the initiative, just relax, listen and give others the opportunity to think of solutions. It sometimes requires me biting my tongue though and I need lots of self-discipline. But it helps me to be considerate to others. You know, you and I are very good in enthusiasm, and we could learn more about listening to others," I conclude the story about my own teachable moment.

"Do you reckon that you could just be a participant in Harry's game?" I say to Daniel. He has listened with great attention and thinks he can manage that. Off he goes to join his friends again. He is so resilient!

DO: Sharing teachable moments is one of the ways to help your child develop virtues. I use it often and learn from it myself. We learn from our mistakes and every teachable moment offers the chance to develop a virtue. It doesn't matter if you or young or older.

Gratitude is very nice

Daniel prefers to wear sports clothes, that is tracksuits, and trainers of a particular brand. I don't really like that last bit, and wonder why these brands matter, but I let it be. Other children also wear them and I understand he wants to look like his friends. It shows a need to practice unity which is also a virtue! I notice from the way Daniel moves that he likes his clothes. It gives him self-confidence.

But ... it is getting cold and I feel those lycra trousers are too thin. I saw some nice warm winter clothes in town and go out to buy him soft corduroy trousers and some polar fleece sweaters. When Daniel comes home from school I show him the clothes and ask his opinion. To my surprise he shows enthusiasm. He puts on one of the sweaters immediately and goes outside to play and show off. I am pleased that I got him the right gear. At night when I go to say goodnight to Daniel, I notice he has neatly folded the sweater and put it on his chair.

I say: "You did a tidy job folding your new sweater." To which Daniel replies: "It's nice of you that you bought me new warm clothes. I am grateful for that and I wanted to show it. The jeans you bought me earlier were not so nice. They have this little pocket on the knee with a tiny nail and that scratches me when I'm running. These trousers are really soft. Will you choose one so I can wear it tomorrow with my new fleece?"

I get another cuddle and am glad that my son can express and voice his gratitude so well. Thankfulness is a very pleasing virtue.

~~~~~~

DO: Enjoy the lovely qualities your child shows you. Allow your thankfulness, love and joy to touch you deeply and give each other a big cuddle!

~~~~~~

Sharing family stories

I often have to tell Daniel the story of his auntie Mary when she was little. She dropped a cake on purpose in a shop because grandma had told her: "Careful you don't drop it!" The 'rebellious' auntie Mary let it drop straight away. "On purpose?" asks Daniel. Grandma thought so, yes. She was embarrassed, and could see people were thinking: "Well, your daughter showed you up!" Daniel thinks that's a good joke, and quite courageous of auntie. Just doing something like that! He can also see the humor of it. He respects his auntie anyway because she just goes ahead and does stuff! She is an example of self-confidence for Daniel.

Sharing with your child stories from your family - or asking their grandparents to do this - encourages your child to think of unity, being part of an extended family and its history. Children recognize qualities that they have inherited from parents or grandparents. They also learn to recognize qualities that they may like to develop. Family stories are full of teachable moments, especially when seen in the context of virtues. And they are often full of humor.

Daniel likes to tell stories, for example about when he was little or what he wants to be when he grows up: currently an estate agent or poet. Listening to your child with respect acknowledges the spiritual warrior in him, the awareness and spirit that is awakening in him.
Daniel's grandma often has to tell him about that time she was given a book from Santa Claus. She had already read the book, long before she got it. How did she do that? She knew where her mom had hidden the present and would read a few pages every day. Every time she had nicely rewrapped the book so that no one would notice. Daniel wants to know: "And then did you act surprised?". He is probably looking for grandma's honesty. "Yes," says grandma, "because I didn't want to hurt my mom and I was also grateful for the lovely book." From his grandma's story Daniel learns about honesty, consideration and thankfulness. Like his grandma, he appreciates things of beauty. Both are very generous, and enjoy giving other people self-made presents and surprises. A nice piece of jewellery or flowers are patiently and lovingly chosen.

With regard to my course participants Daniel wants to know how much I earn. Recently he commented that I should ask for more: "You put a lot of work into this and your participants should appreciate that. You should not be too moderate." He clearly has granddad's confident, determined, purposeful commercial way of thinking! As you can see I can easily identify some virtues in Daniel which I can trace back to my parents and myself or vice versa.

The mystical side of life

Children see the world in a mystical way. They honor heroes and dare to dream big. They like rituals and believe in mysterious beings such as gnomes and witches. For a long time Daniel had a gnome friend with whom he talked daily. At first this gnome friend helped him when he was afraid in the loo. The gnome sat on the sink and chatted to Daniel which made Daniel forget that he was scared to be alone.

According to a remedial teacher friend having an imaginary friend is very healthy. She says: "Children learn to have dialogues with these imaginary friends (whether it's a puppy or a gnome), reflect on events in their life, and pour out their hearts without being judged. A friend like that can also help making moral decisions."

*It can be nice to talk to
an imaginary friend.*

Children can tell you strangest things. When Daniel was three years old, he told me he wanted to be buried on his stomach. Can you picture it? It's literally back to the start!

A few days after a conversation about death and the soul, he informed me: "I can sometimes hear your soul, even if I am not near you..." I am still curious as to what he talking about, some sort of telepathy?

A friend told me that her son had said, just in passing, that he had been her granddad before. She had wondered about that comment because she dearly loved her granddad who had died only days before the birth of her son.

After I had finished teaching my first virtues course I told Daniel - who was four at the time - that I missed it now that it was finished. He looked at me and said: "Sometimes when something ends, it's only starting." And so it turned out to be, I have been providing training and workshops for several years and have initiated the Dutch version of the Virtues Project...

Having a baby is in itself a miracle, but the miracles just keep coming after that. The way your child breathes, drinks, and sleeps. The first steps. The first encounter with a cat or dog.

As a parent you learn, together with your child, to experience wonder again and look anew at things, with attentiveness and respect. It is the ultimate way to slow down and reflect on who you really are.

Cleaning up

When you are working with virtues in your family, you are automatically engaging with the deeper meaning of life. The virtues are part of that because they are part of how you shape your life and your ideals.

We live south of the town in a green neighborhood. A wonderful area to live in, with an easy walk to a lake. Walking, canoeing and cycling. It's just like a holiday spot. Unfortunately on my walks I often spot a lot of rubbish, mainly empty tins or bottles. Not always, but quite often, I pick up what I can and put it in the bin at home.

I do this out of respect for nature and to show Daniel an example of environmental responsibility. I want to instill in him a sense of thankfulness and unity: this planet is not just for our use, it also belongs to future generations, to animals and to plants. Of course it would be best if everybody cleans up their own mess, but if each one of us occasionally cleans up, that too contributes to a greater good: a cleaner environment.

Children often enjoy contributing to this, in their own way. Like any-body, they derive meaning from it and makes them feel they are making a difference, and are being of service.

That feeling is our motivation to clear up wandering rubbish. An-other reason is that we think it looks ugly.

Daniel enjoys talking about this - the environment, climate change, reducing our use of electricity or water - especially now that he is a bit older. He does not think I am moralizing or preachy. I think this is because we keep our discussions light-footed and don't express my views too definitely. I also show him I'm interested in his opinions.

You can take your own look at how you could contribute as a fam-ily to the larger community, the environment around you, and the world. Irene and her three children are putting on an exhibition next month of the drawings and other art works they all made during the holidays. The money raised will go to the charity 'Warchild'. I think it is a great idea. Sonja and her daughters collected signatures when their local pet farm was threatened with closure. The children were completely engaged. They took up this challenge with so much en-thusiasm and idealism, it was brilliant just to watch them. It is won-derful if you can give your child that experience of the virtues of idealism and service while they are still young.

Respect for the dead

At the beginning of the year Tim comes to play. He lives in the next street and attends a different school. They sometimes play together until they have had enough of each other for a while. Very honest and matter-of-fact, the way children can be with each other.

"How old are you Tim?" asks Daniel. He is one year older and likes to emphasize this. "I will be eight in April," answers Tim. He ignores the fact that Daniel shows some contempt. "I didn't celebrate my birthday last year, remember? My cat had just died." Daniel remembers. "I came to the funeral," he says. Tim nods enthusiastically: "Yeah, I remember." He visibly enjoyed the occasion, perhaps more than the birthday party that was canceled. After some reflection Daniel adds: "Remember that I didn't come and play with you for two days?" With a solemn voice he adds: "After all, it's not respectful to play computer games when your cat has just died."

The cat receives a special,
respectful funeral.

We all have to laugh. We're imagining having fun playing shoot-'em-ups on the computer straight after a funeral? No, that does not go together. It is not respectful, or at least it's something that needs some quiet time for thought.

Again I am pleasantly surprised about the ability of these children to think deeply - reflect - about what is respectful and what is not and how this affects their actions. The feeling of respect is a natural one. The event of the cat's death awakened it. To me, that's lovely!

Where were you?

Daniel is back from school. "How was your day?" I ask. "Really nice", Daniel says. They have had a history lesson with just his group. Daniel has only been in this group for a few weeks and reckons it's the best group he's been in so far. Of course he knows that it is not 'cool' to like school, and he moans about the homework. It is incredible how many tasks he is given to do every week. "Especially if you compare it with groups three and four who don't have to do anything… They're just chatting to each other," says Daniel. It drives him nuts. That is why he likes history in Friday afternoon. The 'little ones' leave at noon and group five continues until three PM. Finally they can do some serious work without interruption!

A few months ago we've read Daniel the book Crusade in Blue Jeans by Thea Beckman. So, he knows a lot about the Middle Ages now. And the Dutch 'Golden Age' becomes alive with the book The Cabin-boys of the Bontekoe by Johan Fabricius. The children in these books are independent at a young age. A hard life without parents to look after you, but adventurous.

Daniel cycles to and from school on his own since the start of this school year. I only join him for companioning if he asks me. I can see his confidence grow. I only pick him up on Tuesdays when he has Phys ed in another building. At least, that's the arrangement. One day I am still completely immersed in my work when I hear Daniel enter the house. He immediately shouts upstairs: "Hey mom, where were you?"

I look at the clock on my computer: it's half past three already, I lost track of time. "O my gosh, I completely forgot to pick you up," I say. I'm shocked, and feel like a really bad mom. How could I let this happen?

Fortunately Daniel is not so upset. He comforts me by saying: "It's OK mom, but are we clear that you'll come and get me next time please?" This time he waited fifteen minutes because if he had gone home straightaway, I might have missed him. Good thinking! I am pleased that Daniel did not panic. We agree that he can also come home on his own from this other building. And so I get to practice some detachment - letting go - again, and Daniel has gained more self-confidence.

Hey mom, where were you?
O, gosh, I lost track of time.

Enough is enough

'Enough is enough' is a clear and effective affirmation I have taken from the Family Virtues Guide, where it describes Moderation. More requests for sweets or biscuits by Daniel or his friends is answered by "Enough is enough", providing a clear boundary which is accepted without problems. It's still a challenge for me, a great chocolate lover, to set a good example of moderation! And how about smoking? "You can have one cigarette a day, if that relaxes you," decides Daniel, both for me and himself. He monitors this, not rigidly, but in a detached way. I once again realize that I can learn a lot from him. Will I be able to be so detached when he is old enough to go to the pub and discovers beer?

We both indulge sometimes: Daniel after Halloween,
when he has collected a bag full of candy;
and mum treats herself to a cigarette after a busy day.

The fridge is often a good spot to display
an affirmation, an inspiring quote.

The use of affirmations

In the previous story I showed how to use an 'affirmation'. Affirmations are just short quotes you can think of, write down or speak. Affirmations can be very positive, but also negative. "Enough is enough" is a positive affirmation for us. It helps us, when needed, to exercise moderation. "I can't do it", or "I'm not interesting" are thoughts which can be very negative, beliefs that limit you.

Sometimes, without realizing, you use negative affirmations, for yourself ("I'll never get this!"), for your children ("Stop being so noisy all the time!") and others ("That's way too hard for you"). You can use the virtues to create positive affirmations. They can help you to practice certain qualities!

You can find examples on the Virtues Cards, like the following:

- "I learn from my mistakes" (humility)
- "I speak the truth" (honesty)
- "I let go of negative thoughts" (detachment)
- "I forgive others and myself" (forgiveness)
- "Joy gives me wings" (joy)
- "I bend but do not break" (flexibility)
- "I go with the flow" (grace)
- "Step by step" (patience)

It is best to formulate an affirmation like you're already there: "I am honest", instead of "I want to be honest". That's because our subconscious mind takes things literally and we might end up always wanting to be honest but never being honest.

When creating an affirmation, make sure it is not too rigid. For example: "I do everything step by step and never lose my patience", would be unrealistic in my case. It would be more effective to say: "Showing patience makes me peaceful".

I play on the computer with moderation

Daniel is talking to his dad on the phone and explains enthusiastically about a computer game. He knows he finds it very difficult sometimes to stop playing, it's so much fun. But he reckons that's getting a bit nuts, too. I'm only half-listening to the conversation when I suddenly hear Daniel mention all sorts of virtues: "I am moderate when playing computer games," he tells his dad. "I could play for hours but I'd rather not do that. I control myself. I don't want to become like Tim. Man, he really can't stop and he's always whining if he can play for another hour. He just doesn't want to do anything else anymore. Me, after a while I have played enough."

*I play on the computer with
moderation.*

'Enough is enough!' Daniel clearly picked up on this affirmation and made it his own. I was not aware we've been focusing on it particularly but apparently I'm using it more regularly than I thought. Another time it is Daniel who reminds me of it. I am busy and getting a bit stressed. At some point Daniel questions me about it: "Do you still enjoy what you're doing? Shouldn't you use a bit more moderation in your work? Enough is enough, mom." So cute, the way he looks after me. And tactfully, too. He is correcting me, using the language of the virtues which has become second nature for him!

I think I know all the virtues by now

Speaking about tactfulness: a little while ago Daniel said to me: "Mom, I think I now know all the virtues by now." It was just after running a course, which tends to re-focus me on acknowledging virtues I see around me. I am probably overdoing it for Daniel, which might make it feel not genuine to him, or at least over the top. I have to watch it and keep searching for the right balance. On one hand I want to continue using the language of the virtues regularly. On the other hand I must not overdo it because then it doesn't feel genuine anymore. Here also, the motto is: 'Enough is enough', quite simple actually.

I am convinced the virtues stay active within us, whether or not we are naming them all the time. I hear them every day, also in the way Daniel talks. Last week he commented on a computer game: "Soldiers fight peacefully in this game." After a fight with Harry, Daniel says: "Now it's Harry's turn to make up. I am very steadfast about that." Or talking about a boy dismissed from school because he was always losing his temper: "I think he'd be better off at a self-control school." But Daniel can also mention several good qualities of the dismissed boy, and he reckons the dismissal was not fair: "They should also look at themselves, at how they treat children. That would be more just."

You might think it's too cocky or precocious if a child is reasoning like that. I personally think it shows a lot of wisdom, or rather, awareness.

I think I know all the virtues by now!

Final thoughts on Part 1

The first part of this book has shown how you can use the virtues approach in your life. In the second part of the book you will find a list of virtues, the five strategies of the Virtues Project - ways to help develop the virtues in your children and yourself - and lastly, ideas and exercises for using the virtues approach, such as suggestions for reading stories and virtues-based games.

I am grateful that the Virtues Project entered our lives. Both Daniel and I have developed a great deal of self-confidence and resilience as a result.

Using the positive approach of the Virtues Project we have learned to regard our 'mistakes' as opportunities for virtue development, and we usually can quickly find and develop the missing virtue within ourselves. This balances us.

My heart-felt gratitude goes to the founders of this powerful project. I am grateful to the men in my life - the big and the small one - for the mirrors they have held up to me, the learning moments I have shared with them, and their pride and confidence in me while I was writing this book. I would also like to thank everybody who has so generously helped in making this a good-looking book. Special thanks go to Marianne Offereins for her corrections and suggestions. I am also very grateful to Ineke Gijsbers and Charles Lips for paying so much loving and caring attention to the translation of my book in English.

PART 2: WORKBOOK

Page

Exercises with the five strategies:

Extra information:

Five strategies of the Virtues Project

These strategies - principles - help you to live with respect and pur-posefulness; grow moral awareness in your child; support and guide children's social and emotional development in schools, and in-crease integrity at work. All over the world, people use these strate-gies to create a safe society.

Strategy 1: Speak the language of the virtues

Language is the vehicle of our thoughts. The language of the virtues awakens spirituality. It helps to shape character qualities. The way in which you speak and the words you use, have the power to either discourage or inspire. When you start using the virtues in the lan-guages of your thoughts and of your speech, you will change your relationships. It helps you to replace blaming and shaming language with respectful and uplifting language. You take personal responsi-bility and show respect to others. The language of the virtues brings out the best in yourself and others. It helps you to become the per-son you want to be.

Strategy 2: Recognize teachable moments

You support the development of character in your child, in others and yourself by regarding all daily events as opportunities and chal-lenges, or as teachable moments. When you can learn with confi-dence and humility from your mistakes, every stumbling block be-comes a stepping stone.

Strategy 3: Set clear boundaries

Virtues-based boundaries are aimed at respect, restoration of justice and at the question: "how can we put this right?" Virtues-based boundaries create a safe and peaceful environment. Personal boundaries help you to maintain healthy relationships. They protect your time, energy and health.

Strategy 4: Honor the spirit

First of all this means you respect the dignity of every individual. This strategy also stimulates you to free up time each day to reflect, enjoy the beauty of nature, and express your creativity in art, music or literature. Celebrating special events and the sharing of stories are also good ways to connect with the deeper meaning of your life.

Strategy 5: Spiritual companioning

By intense, fully concentrated presence and listening with compassion and detachment from your own opinions, you will listen to the other person. This simple counseling method uses questions to 'clear the air' and get to the heart of the problem. When someone shares companioning with you, you're offered the opportunity to investigate a teachable moment and to reflect on the virtues called for at that moment. It helps moral decision making and provides intimacy in relations. It is also a powerful tool to heal sadness, anger and traumas.

The use of virtues reflection cards

Picking a random virtue card is an exercise you can do on your own or with others. You use the virtue cards and increase your understanding of every virtue.

Pick a virtue card for yourself

Set aside some regular time for reflection. Randomly pick a virtue card and read it. What speaks to you? What touches you? What moves you? What inspires you? What are you invited to do? What affirmation do you receive? How would this virtue benefit you? By asking yourself such reflective questions you clarify to yourself how to express this virtue in your life. There is a good chance then that the virtue will stay with you for a while, in your thoughts and actions. You will find you recognize the virtue in others now that you understand it better. Do acknowledge it when you see it. This brings the virtue into others' awareness, too.

Pick a virtue card with others

You can do this with others, with your children, partner, friends or colleagues. Pick one card together or have each person pick one. Read the card(s) aloud or silently. One by one mention what this particular virtue means to you. You can share the story of when you used the virtue or saw someone else using it. You can reflect on what the virtue could give you, or how it could help you. You can decide together that each one talks about their virtue without interruption, or you can agree that everyone can add their insights.

DON'T: judge yourself or others. It happens to everyone: you pick a card and read about something you should have done but didn't. Well, too bad. Don't take the card text as an accusation, but rather as an invitation to use the virtue next time - in a similar situation. You'll be more aware of the choices you have then. Do not be ashamed and do not feel guilty. Respect yourself as well as others!

DO: The virtues cards can be useful when explaining the meaning of a virtue to a child. Use your own words if your child does not yet understand the words used on the card. Try to give examples from your own life about the application of this virtue.

Speak the language of the virtues

Hearing from others about your good qualities you show gives you self-confidence and resilience. It tells you who you are.

Naming virtues

Giving a virtues acknowledgement works like this: you name the specific virtue you appreciate or admire in the other, and then you tell them how that virtue showed itself to you. You can also do this the other way round, whichever suits you.

Examples:

"I notice your **patience** when you help your little brother getting dressed."

"I appreciate it that you talked to me so **kindly** and **patiently**."

"You showed **friendliness** when you showed the new kid next door around."

"You showed **helpfulness (or cooperation),** when you gave me a hand with doing the dishes."

"Thank you for your **kindness** in helping me pick up the papers I dropped."

"That was **assertiveness,** when you stood up for yourself, telling me you don't feel like playing football today."

"Did you pack your schoolbag for tomorrow, in order not to forget anything? That's both **responsibility** and **purposefulness**!"

Naming the effect

You can show further appreciation of another's use of a virtue by naming the effect it had on you or others. This is not specifically mentioned in the virtues books from Linda Kavelin Popov, so I'll give some examples here, extending the examples above:

"I notice your patience when you help your little brother with getting dressed". You add: *"It makes him be more helpful himself. Look, he's holding out his arms to help you put on his coat."*

"I appreciate it that you talked to me so kindly and patiently." You add: *"Now I can see how this thing works, and I can use it straight away. Thank you!"*

"You were friendly when you showed the new kid next door around." You add: *"You helped him feel at home here. Did you see how much he enjoyed making new friends?"*

"You were helpful when you gave me a hand with doing the dishes." You add: *"That felt much nicer than if I had to do it alone. We now have a more time to play badminton, let's go!"*

"Thank you for your kindness in helping me pick up the papers I dropped." *You add: "I was so worried they would blow away. It was a great relief when you started helping."*

Start with acknowledging virtues in yourself

You can start with naming the virtues that you yourself show. This may sound a bit strange but it is a very instructive exercise. You don't have to do it out loud. Count your blessings: write them in a small diary every day. This is also good for your self-esteem!

"I showed *understanding* when I listened to my son when he told me he was anxious about... It helped me see how I could help him."

"I was **assertive** when I said that it was a bit too much to drop off as well as pick up the children from football. Another parent then offered to pick the children up."

"I was **patient** and I showed **courtesy** when my colleague became angry. I got a better **understanding** of his problem because I let him talk about it."

"I showed **determination** when Daniel wanted to buy some marbles. He understood when I explained that we can't buy everything we want and he got over his disappointment quite quickly."

"I showed **flexibility** when the children asked if they could play with the garden hose. It felt **joy** when I saw how much fun they had."

Name virtues in your children

You can also start to name or describe virtues you notice in your child. It is like giving a compliment, but more specific. So, don't say: "That's nice" when your child helps you with tidying up. Rather name the virtue of helpfulness, plus how that virtue was practiced. "It was nice that you helped tidying up. Thank you for being so helpful. We're all done already!" Name the virtue when you see your child practicing one spontaneously!

Wrong types of acknowledgements

"You're *always* so helpful", "You're *always* so courageous!": these are examples of incorrect use of the language of the virtues. After all, a virtue is not a permanent state. If you say that someone is courageous, you could imply that they should always be courageous. It's better to say: "I admired your courage with the vaccination. It's pretty scary to get a needle stuck in you. You were nervous, but you went calmly in the queue, and you were trusting as you waited until it was finished."

Do not just say: "You show so much patience, courage, trust etc." without specifying how they showed them. You would overload your child with virtues, and they'll feel stifled.

Be sincere: children know it straight away if you praise their determination while they are not showing it at that moment. Only acknowledge when you really observe your child practicing a virtue.

Be moderate: don't overdo it. You don't have to acknowledge every single occasion that your child is being helpful. Your appreciation can also be shown with a thumbs-up sign, a smile or a quick hug.

"You should be more patient/ confident/ responsible ..." When you say this, you are judging or advising. You may well be right, but it is not the way to awaken virtues in a child. In spite of your good intentions, saying it this way will make the other feel small, guilty or ashamed ("I'm doing it all wrong", or "I'm not good enough"). Try it out, you will notice that any positive message tends to get lost. It's better to look for the virtues your child is showing. See also the 'virtues balance' exercise on page 142.

DON'T: A course participant told me I should have more self-confidence. I knew she meant well. She had enjoyed the course and was pleased with the way I had facilitated it.

DO: I thanked her for her honesty and asked her what she enjoyed most and to name those virtues. She mentioned a whole list: enthusiasm, respect, truthfulness and honesty: "You make yourself vulnerable and that encourages honesty in the participants. No one was judged, everybody was valued." She could specify when I had shown certain virtues. "That gives me confidence," I replied and thanked her for her acknowledgement. Do you see what I did? 1) Appreciating; 2) guiding; 3) thanking...

Recognize teachable moments

Awaken the virtues. Discover something valuable and enjoyable in every child. Every child needs that interested, caring, and loving look which indicates: "I see you, because you are important to me."

Guide your child with the virtues

I always try to look for what is already there, which virtues are being shown by children - people - and name those (see the examples in the previous section). Sometimes you can stimulate the other person a bit and gently guide them in practicing that quality. Let's call that 'awakening a virtue':

"How could you help feeling our new neighbor more at home? Would it be **friendly** to ask him to play marbles with you?"

"I need someone who is willing to be of **service**. I just dropped all my papers. Joshua, please can you help me? Thank you, that was very **helpful**."

"I like to hear your opinion. You're allowed to show some **determination** when you tell me what you think, you know. That helps me to pay attention to your opinion."

Correct your child with the virtues

This goes a step further than just 'awakening the virtue'. You clearly indicate which virtue you think is missing in *this* situation. You remind them of this virtue. You thank the child for adjusting its behavior:

"Please be **considerate** of your brother's feelings; I can see he feels hurt. Thank you for being **tactful**."

"What would help you to be **respectful** to each other?"
"What would be a **friendly** and **tactful** way to say that?"

"I can listen better to you if you talk in a **friendly** manner. Thank you for your **respect**."

Children are often so preoccupied with their own things that they're completely unaware of the effect their behavior has on others. You can remind them by simply mentioning the 'forgotten' virtue: "Michael, look where you throw the sand, so you can **be considerate** of Jenny. See, there's enough room for everybody!"

*In his enthusiasm Michael forgets
to be considerate of Jenny*

Practicing with the virtues balance

I always use an exercise I call 'The virtues balance' in every introductory workshop I do. I learned this exercise from Nancy Watters*, Nancy facilitates Virtues Project courses in Canada.

I ask the parents to name behaviors of their children that annoy them or that they worry about. Very often answers include: "Max can be so stubborn", "Harry is so rude", "Missy is very shy", "Tamara is so messy", "Thomas has no self-confidence", or "Cindy is such a slow-coach". I then ask the parents to discern which virtues their children are showing with these 'undesirable' behavior, and to name virtues could be stimulated.

As in the table on the next page I ask what behavior is undesirable (column 1); What virtue does the child show with this behavior (column 2); Which virtue can balance it all out (column 3).

* www.nancywatters.com/virtuesconsulting.

The virtues balance:

I have deliberately added question marks to the virtues in the 2nd and 3rd columns because this, of course, depends on each individual child and every unique situation.

The unwanted behaviour: my child is so...	The virtue shown by the child; the intention of the behaviour:	The virtue to be developed by the child:
bossy, she dominates other children	enthusiasm? initiative? purposefulness?	respect consideration? patience?
stubborn, goes on until he gets his way	determination? enthusiasm? perseverance?	obedience? flexibility? consideration?
rude, she talks back and butts into arguments	justice? assertiviness? openness?	respect? friendliness? detachment?
shy, she doesn't speak to other children on her own initiative	peacefulness? modesty? dignity?	self-confidence? friendliness? curiosity?
lazy, he avoids chores	detachment? trust? assertiviness?	helpfulness? self-control? responsibility?
chaotic, she's very untidy and leaves a mess behind her	detachment? creativity? enthusiasm?	tidyness? caring? (for things) consideration?
clingy, he is always hanging around me and wants to help me all the time	helpfulness? trust?	respect? (for boundaries) consideration? (other children may want to help too)?

Replace labels by virtues

Think about the labels you have been given by others in your life, or that you have given yourself. In what situations did that happen? What has been the effect? Which virtues could you use to replace these labels? Which virtues do you have, or could you develop, to create a better balance?

As a child I was called 'easy'. I was a lot easier to deal with than my older sister who took some convincing to do things if she didn't feel like it or did not see the point. My parents often sang my praises because I was so 'easy'. The effect has been that I, as an adult, still struggle to voice my opinion: I don't want to be 'difficult'! Within the framework of virtues, I showed a lot of flexibility, was considerate to others, and was willing to be of service. The virtues I am working on now are assertiveness, helpfulness to myself, being considerate to myself as well as others. My sister (the rebellious auntie Mary who let a cake drop in part 1 of this book) is working on grace and gentleness. From her I learn about detachment (letting go, taking a step back). She says: "You can never please everybody."

*Before you know it, you will be stuck
with a label for the rest of your life*

My partner Alex was known as the 'absent-minded professor' in his youth. He easily forgets things because he gets preoccupied with his thoughts. He therefore struggles to remember his commitments and lets things become messy around him. His parents might have helped him practicing orderliness and purposefulness with him. Fortunately he has discovered these himself now. He sometimes still hides behind his nickname and this makes me feel that he is avoiding his responsibilities - if I am not wearing my 'virtues glasses'! In case Alex forgets appointments I try not to get angry but ask him what he can do to remedy the situation. This way I leave responsibility with him, while I get to practice my detachment and tolerance.

The virtues approach is not just good for our personal growth, but also has a positive effect on our relationship. We discover personal and joint teachable moments. Instead of criticizing each other, we discover virtues that can be developed.

Absent-minded professor?
Daydreaming? Or idealistic?

Some more examples:

Your children are doing artwork together; one of them is being 'bossy':

Instead of saying: "Stop being bossy", say: "I see that you're enthusiastic and determined. Would you like the others to accept your idea? How can you be considerate and make sure that the others can also share their ideas? When you consult and cooperate with each other, together you can make something really beautiful!"

Your son is playing on the swing and doesn't want to come inside:

Instead of saying: "Stop whining all the time", say: "I can see you're determined to play a bit longer. You do enjoy your swing, don't you? But now it is time for dinner, and that means we go inside. I (or rather 'the situation') require your obedience now. This means that you listen to my request and come inside with me. Thank you for your flexibility, now we can eat together."

Your daughter often interferes in disagreements and gives rude answers when you ask what has happened:

Instead of saying: "Don't be so rude!", say: "I can listen to you better if you talk to me in a friendly way. Can you show some respect and tell me calmly what happened? … What did you think was not fair? … I'm glad I listened to you and heard your story. I noticed your self-discipline in not swearing. Well done!"

Getting used to the language of the virtues

Mina's parents think she is shy. "But, she has a lot of self-confidence when skating," says her mom Lisette. "She taught herself. She is showing a lot of self-confidence there. I could acknowledge that much more."

The language of the virtues might sound rather stilted and - especially in the beginning - won't come naturally, but you will soon be amazed by the result. Try it out! Think of how our lives will expand we get rid of those labels and interact with each other in a positive way.

Mina shows lots of confidence
when she's skating

Investment of time and effort

Initially, parents are often skeptical and worried that getting into the virtues will take a long time.

Well, especially in the beginning it will require your full attention, and thus time and effort. However, once you are getting used to it, it will hardly take more time and in the end, your interactions with your children will require less effort and energy than they did before. Recognizing teachable moments and approaching your child's behavior in a positive way is in the long run much more efficient than for example grumbling and complaining a thousand times with little effect. That is what really drains your time and energy.

When you can recognize the virtues in your child's behavior, and can suggestions for the ones that are missing, you are investing in your child's self-confidence and sense of responsibility. You will also be building a strong and lasting bond between the two of you.

Over time, the virtues way will become a part of you, and feel quite natural. It won't be an effort anymore to be a virtues educator. That role will be like your favorite coat, which you just slip into without thinking. And as with learning a new language: practice makes perfect. The more you speak the language of the virtues, the sooner it will become your habit.
When you forget, and slide back into judging and advising, you will soon notice the difference: the change in your child's reactions, the restlessness of your thoughts, the feeling in the house. At such times just picking up a virtue card or doing the virtues balance exercise usually helps.

Exercise: self-reflection on the virtues

Think about the labels you put on others or
yourself. Which virtues can you use to replace
these labels? Which virtues can you work on
to find a better balance? If you do this regularly, you will increase your self-knowledge.

Accepting your own unique nature

Thich Nhat Hahn, a famous Buddhist monk and peace teacher, talks
in his book Peace Is Every Step* about the word 'suchness', which
is used in Buddhism to indicate a person's qualities or 'true nature'.

Thich Nhat Hahn says: "If we want to live in peace and harmony
with others, we will have to recognize the uniqueness of everyone.
The key for peace is acceptance. If you do not accept or value the
other person, you will damage your relationship. Negative thoughts
are like clouds before the sun. They overshadow your power to love
and accept.

In Buddhism, we talk about suchness. It is the nature of a person or
a thing. When we understand a person's suchness, we can begin to
love and help him. A person has flowers and garbage within. When
we love, we accept both. It's like a cylinder of gas. We know that gas
is dangerous, but it cooks a good meal. We can live peacefully with
it because we know the suchness of it.

So it is with your wife or husband and children. They, too, have
their suchness, they too have their flower and their garbage. If you
know their suchness, you will be able to live with them happily and
peacefully. You will know how to turn to the flower in them and
you'll profit from that. If you're ignorant, you will turn to the garbage
in them. Therefore, you must understand a person if you want to

* Thich Nhat Hahn: Peace Is Every Step. Bantam Books, 1991

help him and therefore help yourself. Meditation is the practice of nourishing the flower and transforming the garbage to flowers again. It is a continual process. You have to practice it your whole life."

What I learn from Thich Nhat Hanh, is that destructive thoughts can be changed at any moment to a stream of constructive and peace-loving thoughts. You can teach yourself to recognize good qualities - virtues - in others and name these explicitly. As Linda Kavelin Popov says in her book A Pace of Grace*: "Virtues are in the eye of the beholder."

If everybody had something of a Buddhist monk...

* L. Kavelin Popov: A Pace of Grace. Plume Books, 2004

Awakening other virtues through the virtue of acceptance

Practicing the virtue of acceptance will automatically stimulate the practice of other virtues, such as joy, thankfulness, grace, wisdom, tact, detachment - letting go - and trust. Like domino stones, the virtues - your inner qualities - set one another off.

It is easier to enjoy a peaceful and happy life if you accept the unique characters of your children, partner, parents, colleagues and friends, including all their bad habits and highly annoying ways. Imagine waking up in the morning feeling grateful for what you have in your family or relationships, and letting go of your dissatisfaction about what you don't have?

This does not mean that you stop asking for what you need from the other or that you give up your sense of justice, for instance about sharing household chores. If you want your partner or children to be cooperative and helpful, be assertive and explain what you need from them. This is much more efficient than nagging or grumbling. Acceptance does not mean you give up what you think is important; it means you accept people as they are.

Two other exercises in self-reflection

Think: What individual traits do you have, and your children and your partner? Which virtues do you, and they, show with these characteristics?

Try to change angry words or irritated thoughts into shows of affection and encouragement. Ask yourself three simple questions: Am I right in what I think?; Are these words necessary; and lastly: are these ecouraging or stimulating words? Try it and you will see that it works. I have heard that it takes us three weeks to learn a new habit.

Set clear boundaries

Punishing tends to results in guilt and a defensive attitude. State the facts, and ask how things can be made right again, so that both of you can get back on track.

Setting boundaries based on virtues

Many people think of being strict and handing out punishments when it comes to setting boundaries. Setting safe boundaries in the Virtues Project means to define the playground, both physically and mentally. To a toddler who is allowed to play outside on their own, you might say: "You can go as far as that hedge." A child will like this kind of limitation; it is actually getting room to play. It also gives a sense of clarity and security. Virtues can be clear principles for boundaries. Setting boundaries that are based on virtues provides a clearly understandable guideline, both for your children and yourself. It orders your lives. You create calmness for your children and for yourself. You can read how this works from page 161 onwards. First, let's talk a bit more about the importance of safe boundaries and the role of the educator in setting those boundaries.

Authority in the service of a child's learning

Raising a child is described in *The Family Virtues Guide* as 'using authority in service of learning'. You give guidance to your child to help it develop qualities. You help the child to develop its inner authority: the ability to make its own moral choices, and to deal with the consequences of those choices.

The Virtues Project teaches educators to give the child room to develop. But that space has limitations. There are clear boundaries, agreements based on virtues. Both child and parent experience teachable moments within these boundaries. Together they can agree on consequences, for example what happens after forgetting an appointment.

As a spiritual guide you must give up your need to be always popular with your child. You just do your best to guide your child's behavior, honestly and lovingly. Your clear and reasonable discipline will give your child with the basis of self-discipline.

Which parenting style do you have?

The Family Virtues Guide describes four extreme types of parenting: permissive, dominant, democratic and sliding:

Permissive:

Permissive behavior can result in a lack of mutual respect. A permissive parent avoids authority. He or she wants to prevent disappointments for the child, or sometimes moaning from the child. The child does not learn how to deal with disappointments. No boundaries are set. Your child will become confused because you, as a parent, are not being clear about what is right or wrong. Alternatively, your child could become extremely bossy and ruling the household. Children of permissive parents often have - even later in life - difficulties with applying virtues such as moderation, self-discipline and purposefulness. Extreme permissiveness can result in child neglect.

Dominant:

Dominance results in feelings of guilt or shame. A dominant parent, often known as authoritarian, enforces maximal control. "It is because I say so" is often the parent's attitude. A child of a dominant parent is placate and a people pleaser. It learns not to think for itself nor take responsibility for its own actions. It learns not to develop his or her inner compass. It learns not to be assertive. A child reacting against a dominant parent becomes rebellious and disobedient. In both cases children lack self-confidence, a virtue they will miss later in life and which will requires a lot of additional effort to develop. In extreme cases of authoritarian parenting children are suppressed.

Democratic:

Democrats in education can result in confusion about equality. As human beings we are all equal, but your role as an educator is distinctive. A democratic parent does not teach its child a lot about determination. Parent and child can end up in paying attention to everybody (except themselves) and flexibility (disempowerment). Conflicts and power struggles are common in extreme cases of democratic parenting.

Sliding:

Sliding between these three styles can result in a situation in which the child takes control and starts to tyrannize their class mates, siblings or parents: it has too much power and not enough guidance. Often the parent manipulates the situation: changing between bribing, begging, and getting angry. In extreme cases this can lead to complete chaos in families.

A practical example:

Mary was given a pet rabbit for her birthday. She had wanted one for ages and you agreed with her that she would look after it. Bunny needs food and fresh water every day. His cage must be cleaned once a week. Mary has agreed that she will take care of all this.

The first few weeks are fine. Bunny is very well looked after. But after a few months, things aren't going so well anymore. There are so many other nice things demanding Mary's attention! Bunny has not been fed nor has his cage been cleaned.

How do you think about how the four 'extreme' parents would handle this situation? And then: how would you?
Would the permissive parent do it herself? What about the dominant parent? That one is likely to threaten and think of a punishment. The

democratic parent will gets preachy and keeps nagging about the problem until they get into a big argument. The sliding parent tries to bribe Marie into cleaning the cage: "You can play outside a bit more after this." Assuming Marie does not go for that, the parent might switch to begging, preaching, nagging or - if still without success - take harsh actions: "The rabbit is going, you don't deserve to have one if you don't look after it." Wasted are the teachable moments, in all cases. And all completely unnecessary, as a clear agreement had been made with Mary at the start.

The trick is to see the teachable moment. Which virtues was Mary forgetting? Which virtues did Mary use when she looked well after her rabbit? Which virtues do you need yourself in order not to react in a permissive, authoritarian, democratic or sliding manner? Take the time to ponder on this situation, within the context of the virtues. When you have identified the relevant virtues, name them as you talk with your child. In the above example, the parent could remind Mary that she showed so much responsibility and care at the beginning. Then Mary is asked how she can pick up these virtues again. This is done without nagging or preaching, neither is Mary made to feel guilty or ashamed. But the parent is clear and determined: "Mary, we agreed you would look after your rabbit. It went fantastic at the beginning; you were really responsible and caring. What happened this week to make you forget? What can help you to keep to your commitment?"

Make yourself clear

Making yourself clear is not the same as being angry. It is important that you start by taking the child seriously, even if you do not agree with the behavior. This does not mean that you efface yourself. The stronger you are within yourself, the more room you have to spare for your child. Dealing with boundaries is a process in which both children and parents all develop virtues.

Setting boundaries: a challenge for the whole family

With the help of the virtues you can make agreements in your family (or class, or group) which you record in a 'Mission Statement'. This may sound very business-like, but it really works!
Choose several virtues that are important to you. What do you want to pass on to your children? What needs special attention? Let everyone join in with this consultation. Decide together which ideas you want to make into your house rules, that you agree to live by. The virtue cards can lead the way here. Write the agreements on a poster and place this in a handy location where everyone can see it. Children often enjoy decorating this poster with drawings or pictures. Keep it positive and light: the rules are meant to be a challenge.

Principles for house rules

Below you will find some principles for devising house rules. Check them against the examples on the next page:

- House rules are based on virtues: they define the boundaries
- House rules are clear and specific
- House rules indicate what behavior is acceptable
- House rules are made clear to everyone; everyone commits
- House rules are a challenge to deal with another in a transparent and trustworthy way: everyone understands where the boundaries are
- House rules result in safety, both physical as emotional. They help by respecting everyone's need for privacy, space, understanding, and the fair sharing of tasks
- House rules can be adapted over time and depend on ages, possibilities, surroundings: together you think of practical solutions
- House rules are non-negotiable
- House rules are succinct
- House rules are formulated in a positive manner: they tell you what is expected, not what is prohibited.

Safe boundaries:

Joy: we make time for fun and doing nice things together, such as chatting, playing games and walks.

Respect: we accept it if someone needs time for themselves, or wants to be alone, or wants to do something like as going on the computer or reading, or just needs some space.

Understanding: we accept each other as we are.
We listen to each other, even if we disagree or get annoyed.
If we have an argument, we talk about it.

Excellence: we don't have to do everything perfectly or be the best all the time.
We do our best and enjoy the work and play just much as the results.

Tidiness: we tidy up our own clothes, shoes, breakfast, newspapers and toys as much as we can.

Responsibility: we all contribute to household chores and do our jobs on time.

Assertiveness: we don't have to do everything alone.
We ask help when we need it
or if the other can do something for us.

Signed by: Alex, dANiel and Annelies

Determine consequences

As a parent, it is good to realize that small children cannot foresee the consequences of behavior yet. They need your guidance. You, preferably together with the children, and at a time when the negative behavior is not at issue, can consult and agree about consequences for certain behavior. Ensure that the punishment, both in content and severity, fits the misdemeanor. Ask: "What happened?", "What led to it?", "What is the effect?" and "How can it be made up for?" You can consult together about what should be done to put things right. Make sure that the consequences follow soon after the offences and that the reason for the consequence is understood.

Examples of fitting consequences:

If you don't set aside enough of your time for family togetherness, a consequence could be that you have to organize a family outing. If you forget to clear away your breakfast, you need to clear everyone else's as well. If you have forgotten a responsibility, you do it now, even if it is late. You do not get new privileges - like a new bike - until you show you can handle the responsibility - by putting your bike in the shed. Try to match the consequence to the offence. What is important is that you do not punish randomly, for instance by threatening with less TV or earlier bed time. You (jointly if possible) search for a fitting consequence which helps to develop the forgotten virtue.

Be consistent

You can count on children testing boundaries, even after making clear agreements. You can then, plain and brief, remind them of the agreement. This makes your agreements meaningful. It shows that you are a reliable parent and your child experiences what reliability means. I prefer to use 'spiritual companioning' (see Strategy 5) if agreements are regularly forgotten. The motto here is: 'Don't get angry, get curious!' Often some feeling or other reason is hidden behind it. Make sure you get that out into the open. Just punishing, in the sense of unpleasant consequences, is mostly ineffective and only results in shame, guilt and power struggles. A more useful tool is a time-out to cool off and reflect. After this you can ask the child what it needs in order to observe the rule, or how it can make up for not following the rule.

Think of safety

An imposed clear structure is sometimes necessary, so that in all instances the child is clear about consequences of disobeying the rules, and the reasons for this. The disadvantage is that the child misses out on an opportunity to develop its inner compass. However, such a clear imposed structure is essential for children with certain conditions, such as those on the autistic spectrum, or with anti-social or oppositional behavior problems. These children require an external compass, for their own safety and those around them. This is also the case for young children. Therefore observe what your child is capable of at its present age. Adjust your boundaries and expectations to fit the child, and as always be mindful of safety first.

Impose boundaries if the virtues are violated

I often use, in my course, the example of a child hitting somebody with a stick. Should you be thinking about which virtues your child is showing and which ones are needing development then? Do you say: "What an enthusiasm Daniel. Please remember to be gentle!" Of course not. At such times you take the stick away from the child. You take the child to a quiet space and request calmness. The calmer you can remain, the sooner your child will calm down. You can talk when you have both settled down. I would choose for spiritual companioning in this case also: "What happened? What made you hit with the stick?" You open the door and invite the child to express his or her feelings. If the child finds it difficult to articulate these feelings, you can help: "You were swinging that stick pretty wildly... You hit that girl on her head. What made you so angry? How can you handle that anger in a gentle manner? What could you say? How can you control yourself? What can help you?"

Close with a clear task: "That must have hurt her a lot. How can you make up?" and acknowledge a virtue in your child. In this situation you could say: "You have listened carefully and told me about your feelings. I can see that you thought it was unfair she took your bike off you. But that is never a reason to hit someone. I am glad that you want to make it up in a friendly manner, which is very brave of you."

Setting boundaries with the language of the virtues

Setting boundaries based on virtues means talking the language of the virtues. We already talked about this in the paragraph "correcting your child with the virtues" on page 145. You clearly indicate which virtue you think is missing in that particular situation. You remind the other person of that virtue:

"Please be considerate of your brother's feelings, I can see he feels hurt."

"What would help you to be respectful to each other?"

"What would be a friendly and tactful way to say that?"

Stopping dangerous behavior

Dangerous behavior (such as hitting with a stick) is stopped immediately: "Stop that, it is dangerous" and the stick is taken away). If the unwanted behavior triggers strong feelings in you or the other person, it's probably a good idea to take time-out so both can detach and let go of their emotions.

Later you can talk together about why you had these strong reactions. This is often a sign that a virtue is missing. Figuring out which one that is can be done jointly or on your own. Preventing the use of sticks for hitting might require responsibility, or self-control...

Ask the question 'How can you make up?'

When emotions have settled you can ask: "How can you make up?" This is known as 'Rrestorative justice'.

The virtues balance can help you to make a start with restoring justice. You name or more virtues you saw in the (unwanted) behavior of your child and ask what it can do to make up.

Do you remember the virtues balance?
(Page 142)

Honor the spirit

Make a habit of contemplation. Children are mystical by nature. Support children in learning virtues, the basic elements of spirituality. Let them discover the 'spiritual warrior' they truly are in their deepest selves.

Strategy 4 is about contemplation and spirituality, something that used to be expressed in religion and the arts. Nowadays other ways of expressing spirituality are more common. Strategy 4 supports you to be spiritually active, to reflect on the mystery of life and explore its meaning. You can do this for yourself, to maintain your energy and inspiration as a parent. You can do it with your children or the entire family: play sports or games, read, explore nature, paint, listen to music, go to the cinema or a museum, invite friends for meals, have a short holiday, take your son to a football match, take your daughter to Paris for the weekend when she moves to high school…. There are many ways to stop and smell the roses, and experience a special moment together.

Reflection:

How can we 'Honor the spirit'? You can ask yourself, your children or partner the following questions; they can be adapted for all ages:

- How do I apply strategy 4 in my life at this moment?
- How do I do this in my relationship, my family, together?
- Which ideas come up in me?
- What benefits will this give to my relationship, my family?
- How can we create more of these restful and joyful moments?

Boundaries for helping you stay spiritually healthy

Create a daily routine of silence and reverence to pay attention to your spirituality, for instance you could reflect on a virtue card every day - even if it's only a few minutes.

Practice joy: what do you enjoy? What do you enjoy doing together? Make time for friendship, listening, companioning and being together.

Strive for integrity. Be genuine towards yourself and others. Do it now!

Be amazed. Expose yourself to beauty and art. Spend time in nature, an art gallery or a museum.

Painting and drawing brings me back to myself
and gives me joy.

Ideas for 'Honoring the spirit'

The use of Virtues Cards as mentioned on page 133: pick a virtue card and tell what this virtue means to you at this moment in your life, or how you want to practice the virtue. The others listen with respect and in silence.

You can also do a 'virtue pick' by yourself. Another option is to focus on a weekly virtue and keep a diary.

Give yourself (and your partner, children) a virtues acknowledgement at the end of the day.

Count your blessings: keep note of what makes your day, what brings you joy and what you are grateful for. Talk with others about it or write it in your diary.

Seize the day: start your day with a moment of spiritual awareness. The good feeling it gives you will stay with you all day (you might feel too tired if you plan this in the evening).

You can also note down your dreams and ideas. What do you need to achieve your spiritual goals? Which virtues can help you? Which boundaries can help you?

Take turns in describing a magical moment in your life.

You can pass on an imaginary box with a story in it. Open the magic box, tell the story, close the box and pass it on.

You can invite your child to bring things back from nature or explore nature together. Linger a while and wonder at some of the things you see, the beauty we are given, that is just there for us all to enjoy.

Create your own 'altar': a place where everybody can lay a cherished item, like a ring, a cuddly toy, a photo, candle, shells or stones from a holiday, flowers, perfume, a poem, a drawing. You can also add a little tray of candy hearts ('kisses', 'love' etc).

Create a banner on which everybody writes a message. You hang this banner during your virtues meetings.

Make a virtues tree from cardboard, branches, blackboard paint…

Share a cherished memory from your childhood.

Share favourite music. Tell why you chose to share a specific song.

Pass a burning candle around and make a wish, aloud or silently, or say thank you to someone that you are thinking of.

Hide stones in a pot of sand. Take turns digging out a stone. Use a felt-tip pen to write a virtue on it that you want to practice over the coming period. Tell others how you are going to go about that. Carry your stone with you or put it in a special place.

Read or tell a story or poem and make drawings afterwards, so that the story/poem comes alive.

Look at photos or paintings and allow the meaning they have for you to penetrate. Share this.

Talking philosophy with children gives them room to find their core. Let them discover that they can think for themselves and share their thoughts; that there is no right or wrong in this.

Spiritual companioning

Listen fully to the heart, spirit and character of the child. Follow it and ask questions: "How did that feel for you?" and "What can help you?" instead of immediately giving your opinion or coming up with a solution.

Every one of us has had the experience of not being heard or seen, and has experienced the feelings that provokes. Many of us know this feeling from a very early age. Some will react by withdrawing within themselves (imploding), others express their reaction to the outside world (exploding).

Unfortunately what happens very often in our lives as educators is that we repeat the same mistakes as our own educators. In other words: we repeat the same behavioral patterns and let hurry, stress, busy-ness, tiredness, absent-mindedness get in the way of hearing what our children are really saying. Or we walk into the other trap: have you had too much authority imposed on you as a child? Then you might be giving your children too much room. Were you not protected enough in your youth? You may be reacting by being over-protective with your children. All with the best of intentions, by the way. We always want the best for our children.

A lot of frustration and anger expressed by children is caused by this feeling of not being seen or heard enough. Remember how you feel when you're talking about something and the other is not really listening to you. You either stop talking or you might even act silly in order to get the other person's undivided attention. It is a rarity in our hurried lives nowadays to experience being listened to with complete attention. When you experience this, it can feel as if you are gently cleansed within, re-balanced, re-energized.

This is also the case with children. They are born with the capacity to feel all emotions. If these can be listened to, together, they learn gradually that emotions are meaningful, there to tell you something.

They learn that you can act to direct or change your feelings. That you need to convey your feelings, to allow the other to 'see and hear' you. Over the years children learn, by their interactions with their environment, how they can express their emotions so that others know what is happening inside them.

The art of true listening

You will never know what another person feels without true listening. True listening is paying full attention to the other while letting go of your own point of view. This is hard, if not the hardest thing of all. You often think you already know what the other is talking about and have some ideas about solutions. This means that while listening you're not really with the other, but busy associating what you've heard with your own experience. And that was not the point. The other person has a problem and wants a listening ear, wants some help from you to get things clear in their mind, so as to enable them to find their own solutions. The art of listening is about going to stand on the other person's point of view. You don't have to any thinking along, rescueing or advising. You only have to be there for the other, and ask such questions that help the other person get to the heart of the problem. Ask those questions that help the other to come up with their own solutions or next steps.

Listening with compassion and detachment

Companioning is a way to follow your child in behavior and thought, and to stimulate your child to experience awareness of its own feelings without having to feel criticized or judged, without being rescued or directed.

Please refer to the virtues books of Linda Kavelin Popov for more background about this method of counseling. You can find a scheme from the 7 steps of companioning on page 188.

The 7 steps of companioning:

Step 1: Open the door

Be curious. Offer your child the opportunity to talk freely. You can often see your child needs this. Your child is acting angry or moody, or comes home all excited. You can start by asking: "What happened?" This is an invitation for the child to talk. As you can see in the diagram most questions start with "What" and "How". These are the magic words. They help you to ask open questions. "How was school?" or "What did you do?" are examples of open questions. They invite a story. "Was school nice today?" is a closed question. The child just has to answer yes or no and you're done with the conversation.

Step 2: Offer your silence to the other

Give your child space to talk freely. Concentrate fully: be 100% present to your child. Trust in your child's process. Do not interrupt. Do not rescue, guide or advise. Your agenda is empty: you listen with compassion and detachment. You do not guide your child; you walk along with them on the path of their choosing. Allow silences to be there. If you don't get an answer to a question straight away, don't go asking more questions or start filling in what you think your child is feeling. Just calmly wait. Count to ten. If the child isn't getting started with talking, ask questions such as: "What is so difficult to talk about?" or "It seems difficult to find the right words. What could help you? What would you like to say about it?" If a child does not want to discuss it at all, just say: "I have the feeling this is hard for you to talk about. I respect that. I just want you to know that I am glad to listen to you if something bothers you. I trust that you will know the right moment for that."

Step 3: Ask questions that help them get things off their chest and that lead to the heart of the problem

Ask questions starting with 'What', 'How' and 'When'. Not 'Who' and never 'Why'. 'Why' requests an immediate judgement. Show that you're listening by nodding or saying "Uh-huh" or "Mmm". You don't need to understand the details during companioning. You only need to 'be there' so that your child can hear itself. Your child will get to know its own valuable feelings that help it come to decisions about what to do next. Ask questions that help the child clarify their story. Ask questions such as: "How was that for you?" or: "What is the hardest thing about this?" or: "What are you most worried about?" or: "What is it that you don't know?". All these questions hone in on the heart of the matter. You can also use this step separately from all others. Suppose a child says: "This isn't working". You reply: "What's not working?" The child says: "It is too difficult for me to tidy up my own clothes." You reply: "What is too difficult?" The child says: "I can't do it." You reply: "What is it you can't do?" or: "How is that for you?" The child says: "It's hard to get the wardrobe open, and the shelves are too high and that makes me angry." And so, with your guidance, the child has arrived at the heart of the problem: it can go on to find its own solution and implement it.

Step 4: Pay attention to sensory clues

What does your child see, hear or feel? Join in with their sensory experiences. It will make it easier for your child to get to the specific feeling, feel it and let go of it. Reflect feelings, use the clues or words your child gives out. Check: "Does it grab you by the throat?" or: "Does it hit you in the stomach?", or ask more questions: "What's happening deep inside you?" or: "What are you feeling?" or: "What do you see?" or confirm: "That's a sore cut!"

We often tend to analyze problems. Using questions that take their cues from body signals will help your child to focus from the head (analytical) back to the heart (emotional). By naming what you see, you show the other that you hear what they are saying. If your child starts to shift around uncomfortably, you can comment: "Is this making you uncomfortable?" or you can ask: "What would make you feel calm again?"

Step 5: Ask reflective questions focused on virtues

When the cup has been emptied, wait a bit longer. Sometimes another revelation will surface, from a deeper layer. At this stage your child has had the opportunity to listen to itself and clarify its feelings. You can lead a bit more now. Your questions will now focus on helping the other reach a decision about what to do next. Your agenda is still empty though! You just ask questions which will help the other to make a moral decision, based on virtues: "I can hear it's a bit scary. Which virtue can help you now?" or: "What can help you to be less shy?" or: "What else do you need?" or: "What could be a way to solve this problem?" or: "What do you feel is the right thing to do?" and if necessary: "How can I help you?". Ask open questions. Don't offer a virtue because you then nudge the child in your direction, impose your solution: "You can do it with a bit more courage." Ask: "What would make you less unsure or less anxious?" rather than: "What can give you more self-confidence?"

Step 6: Concluding and integrating questions

Ask questions such as: "What has become clearer now?" or: "What is clearer now we've talked about it?". With this you will help the child to integrate thinking and feeling, and wrap up the issue. The heart and the head are knitted together, as it were. Sometimes people feel that this step is like fishing for a compliment that I'm such a great listener or that I am so nice. You can leave that thought, however: step 6 is meant to help the other to summarize what the talk has resulted in, so they can get to work with a clear purpose.

Step 7: Acknowledge virtues

Finish with the acknowledgement of virtues you have seen, heard or otherwise noticed in the course of the conversation: "I heard you talk with respect about your friend" or: "I can see that this decision is a bit scary for you. I admire your courage" or: "You have considered everybody while deciding what to do. You show a sense of justice doing that."

DON'T: Ask questions such as "Who ...?" or "When....?" These are detective questions that are only useful to the guide because the speaker already knows these facts. Those questions often don't lead to the core, the emotions. The "Why?" question causes resistance because you have to justify something. This question does not lead to a solution either.

DO: The most important and most beautiful aspect of companioning is that there are no hidden agendas. You're not making a problem personal. The questions you ask to get to the heart of the problem begin with: "What...?" or "How...?" You trust that your child will discover its own truth as long as you listen fully and ask the right questions. The 7 steps of companioning can also be used independent from each other. Give companioning to yourself, your partner, friend or colleague. It deepens your contacts with others and yourself.

A common reaction when your child has a problem

Let me give a simple example to show what the result is of our usual reaction:

Daniel says: "Mum, I can't do this presentation in class." I could 'rescue' him, give ideas, search topics, put the presentation together. I can advise and guide him: "Look in the library or on the Internet." I can criticize him: "You left it too late, didn't you. Now you're stuck. I would also be nervous if I were like you and didn't have a topic yet." I can gripe: "Oh, now I have come and help? Why didn't you think of that before? Figure it out yourself. I really don't have time now to help with your homework. You should have started much earlier. Oh very well then, what do you want the topic to be?"

These are all likely answers; they look innocent and maybe even helpful. Of course these answers affect your child and your relationship. In any case they give the child the message: "I will do the thinking for you." The child will then either think: "I'm not smart enough to think for myself" or: "Cool, I'll just tag along! I don't have to think myself" or: "Mum always knows better" or: "Gosh, I am a real moron."

If we want to truly support our children we will help them to develop their own inner authority. It's important that you achieve the two following points: you acknowledge that you have heard the child, and you acknowledge that you believe it can figure out its own solution and take care of itself.

An example of companioning

Daniel (angry): "I can't do this. I have to give a presentation to my class, but I just can't do it."
Me: "Oh dear. Tell me, what is the task exactly?"
Daniel (almost crying): "We have to give a 10-minute presentation about a topic we don't know a lot about yet. It's for tomorrow. I

haven't done anything yet."

Me (sympathetic and curious): "What an awful situation! How come you haven't started on it until now?"

Daniel: "It looks so difficult."

Me (after silently counting to at least 10: " … What is the most difficult part?"

Daniel: "The topic. Everybody is talking about their pet. But I think that is stupid and boring."

Me: "Uh-huh … "What would be an exciting topic?" … "How can you find it?"

Daniel (fiddling with his blank piece of paper): "… I would like to talk about earthquakes … but, that's way too difficult."

Me: "… I can see you're nervous because you don't have anything down yet. That blank paper looks pretty bad, doesn't it? What can help you make a start, if it's going to be about earthquakes?"

Daniel (slightly perkier): "I could look on the Internet, search Google for 'earthquakes'."

Me (enthusiastic): "That's a great idea! What else do you need to get going with your presentation?"

Daniel (a bit more enthusiastic): " … I'm OK. I just have to find out a bit more first."

Me (with moderation and detachment): "What has become clearer?"

Daniel: "Perhaps it's not so bad, I just need to get started."

Me: "You look relieved. It's great you were assertive enough to share your worries with me. You're always welcome to ask for help. I can see that you have found your self-confidence to put together a good presentation. Let me know if there is anything else I can do to help you."

Daniel: "OK, maybe I need you to practice on, later…"

Me: "That is fine; just call me when you're ready to practice."

Children's books and story-reading suggestions

My parents read me lots of stories when I was a child. Using all my persuasive skills I could sometimes get them to read me five in a row - showing tact and determination on my part! I think this sowed the seeds for my love of reading. I love books, to me they are a wonderful way to relax. I can be fully immersed in the story and often finish the book in a single reading. And it seems Daniel has inherited this: he also enjoys reading enormously. Since he turned eight, he is reading one book after another. We both still enjoy me reading stories to him, sometimes we'll take turns reading a passage.

In storybooks many qualities
can be found

I think reading stories to children is very important. It stimulates their imagination, develops their feel for language, and it grows their awareness of the virtues. Of all the things you and your child can do together, reading stories is a particularly good way to learn about virtues. Children are open to new experiences even at a young age, including from books, and can learn from these experiences. Besides, it's a great way to have fun together, and at the same time you are practicing strategy 4, 'Honor the spirit'.

Recognize virtues in a story

If you look for them, there are virtues to be found in all books. Since learning about the virtues I have started to name them: "All the little mouse children helped mother mouse when she was ill. That was really helpful!" or: "They went looking for food in the big people's kitchen. How courageous!" or: "Timmy mouse cut his nose while eating from that tin. Sister Minnie quickly tore off a piece of her apron to bandage that poor nose. Wasn't that caring of her?", or a little later, after one of the mice falls in a pot of jelly and the others pull him out with a rope: "Now that's cooperation!". It's good practice for both parent and child to find the virtues in a story.

Recognize teachable moments

The characters in stories make mistakes, just like us. You can realize together that they have their biggest teachable moments when they fall and learn how to get back up. Try looking at those moments from the perspective of virtues: you can learn a lot from that. What choices did the heroes have at an exciting stage? Would you have done the same? What virtues can you see in the heroes? What virtues can you see in the baddies? The older the child, the greater its ability to empathize with characters in a story. Because you are reading the book together, you can discuss all this, and your child learns to reflect on the virtues.

Using stories to reflect on virtues

Daniel and I used to look back on the day during storytelling: "When did we show this quality ourselves today?" You can give affirmations to yourself and each other in this way. "Daniel, you have been such a good help this afternoon. I really liked that. You were so cooperative with Henk when you were building that Lego town."

Daniel has made a game out of finding virtues in a book he is reading. He might tell me how the main character in a book is very steadfast. He might comment on how different the various characters are, and how well they complement each other. He will give me book tips: "For your students!"

More storytelling ideas

Your child will often have its own ideas and feelings about a story, and with a little encouragement will talk about its own experiences as they relate to the story. You can talk about that, and this way your child will stay engaged with the story, put itself in the character's shoes, and become aware of all sorts of qualities.

When you get to a suspenseful moment in the story, you can ask your child what might happen next. Pondering what might happen is a good thinking exercise that helps your children's problem-solving abilities in daily life.

When you get to names for virtues that your child does not know yet, you can help them learn by showing them a picture, or by acting it out, or by giving examples from your own experience: "You showed courage going on that high slide!" In this way, your child will be able to retain the new word better.

Games and ideas for activities

Together with your children you can draw or make something artistic in which the virtues play a role. Think for instance of an origami 'folding flower' with the virtues written on. Or a tree (from cardboard and paint, or from real branches) with fruits representing the qualities. This can be your family virtues tree.

An origami 'folding flower' with
virtues written on the petals.

You can also play word games with virtues like guessing virtues starting with a certain letter. One starting with F would be friendliness. If you have guessed that, you can also do charades with it. Or make a grab-bag with hidden virtues.

Happy, sad, angry, scared game: learn to recognize and express feelings. Give each other companioning. Use cards with facial expressions (happy, sad, angry, scared). You can easily make these yourself. Take turns in telling how you feel and why that is. Ask questions that will help to vent feelings. Ask what can be done to help. Give a virtues acknowledgement.

Virtues hunt: make a grab-bag with questions like the ones below. Each person picks a question and answers it:

- Name three virtues you want to develop.
- Name a virtue you saw at home this week.
- Name a virtue you notice in your partner, neighbor, …
- Name a virtue you needed this morning while getting up.
- Name a virtue you see in your best friend.
- Name a virtue you need when you go to work.
- Name a virtue you need when you're doing homework.
- Name a virtue you need when you travel.
- Name three virtues you like in your friend.
- Name a virtue you can call on when doing the dishes.
- Name a virtue you need when you see something unfair.
- Name a virtue you can call on when you try out something new.
- Name a virtue you don't know a lot about.
- Name a virtue you know a lot about.
- Name a virtue you would like everybody to use.
- * Name three of your favorite virtues.
- Name a virtue you like on your birthday.
- Name a virtue that can turn a bad day into a good one.

Happy, sad, angry, scared game: learn to recognize and express feelings. Give each other companioning. Use cards with facial expressions (happy, sad, angry, scared). You can easily make these yourself. Take turns in telling how you feel and why that is. Ask questions that will help to vent feelings. Ask what can be done to help. Give a virtues acknowledgement.

Design name tags, for instance in the shape of a gem. Provide materials for everybody to design and make their own gem name tag. You can then add virtues to the tag of someone else if you see them practice it (make sure you tell them as well).

Virtues shield: Make a knight's shield from cardboard or wood, and paint your most important virtues and values on it. Older children can make their own shields, while you can give younger children a pre-drawn one to cut out. The children draw a large circle in the center of a cross that fills the shield. The top two quadrants display the names of two virtues that are already well developed in the child. They can add drawings or symbols. The bottom left quadrant could be used, for instance, for 'joy' decorated with something that expresses their joy in life. The bottom right quadrant can display a virtue which is a challenge for the child. This is the virtue that the child wants to cultivate, work at. The circle in the center can be filled with their totem or personal symbol, for instance a horse-shoe if you like horses, an angel wing, a musical note, or whatever speaks to the child.

Virtues collage: make a collage of words and virtues you think are important or want more of in your life.

Notice in newspapers and books which virtues are mentioned. Talk about this with others. Do you know the meaning of that virtue? What is the effect on the characters of using or not using those virtues?

Choose photos or images from newspapers and magazines. They could be of as eagles, children, planet earth, bottles, beautiful objects, people from different cultures or with different facial expressions. Mix the selection, spread them out in the middle of a circle and let each person choose one. Make pairs and talk about what attracted you to that particular image/photo and what is the connection with their personal lives.

Virtues board: everybody chooses a virtue they want to add to the board. Make a collage together which represents the virtue.

Role plays about virtues: every virtue in the Family Virtues Guide lists at least six situations under the heading: 'What would ...... look like?'. Children enjoy recreating these situations. First do the role play without using the virtue, then repeat it with the virtue.

Virtues circle or virtues course

Maybe you enjoy exchanging experiences and thoughts with other parents about the use of virtues with yourself and your children. The Virtues Project encourages everybody to initiate virtues circles. You can start these informally at any time with anyone.

If you want to provide formal courses to parents or trachers, you will need to train as Facilitator and will work within the Facilitator framework. Look on *www.virtuesproject.com* for more information.

What now?

At the end of this book you learned about the virtues and the five strategies. What can you do next? What do you want to do next?

Answer for yourself the following questions. If you know someone else, for instance your partner or a fellow course participant, who has also read the book, maybe you can compare answers and discuss them.

- What is going well in my life? Which virtues have helped me?
- What are my biggest teachable moments? Which virtues can help me?
- What do I feel I would like to do right now with the Virtues Project, in my life, my family or my class?
- How do I want to go about that?
- What concerns or hesitation do I have when I think of that?
- What do I hope will happen?
- Which boundaries do I need? Which virtues will help me?

Make some notes for yourself, and read them again after a few months or a year: where are you now?. This annual review is a great tool for purposeful evaluation and further virtues development.

Frequently asked questions

My book has turned out to be useful to people (parents and teachers) already into *The Family Virtues Guide* or *The Virtues Project™ Educator's Guide*. The practical examples and exercises from Bring out the best in your child and yourself, raising children with the virtues are seen as an addition for bringing out the full potential of the virtues approach in their family or school.

Raising children with virtues is also read by people who do not yet know about the Virtues Project, or those who struggled with using the basic books. I came to the conclusion that all the books and the *Virtues Reflection Cards* can be used jointly or separately.

I have also been asked questions about the structure of the book, and the best way of using it. I have also been asked questions such as: "What are virtues?" and "Are all virtues good?" I will use this paragraph to answer these questions.

What is the best way of using this book?

Raising children with virtues is divided into two parts:

The first part describes my own experiences of the education of my son Daniel and examples from course participants. I have changed all names of participants and children in order to protect everybody. This includes the name of my son 'Daniel'.
Part two is a workbook, with more theory and exercises, to practice the virtues approach.

Sometimes certain aspects became suddenly clear. I'm especially grateful for the many ideas from my colleague Master Facilitator Willy Hensen. She has been engaging with the strategies of the Virtues Project as long as I have and has a lot of experience with teaching in schools and teacher training. I describe our insights in short interludes.

What is the best way to start?

I describe my personal journey of discovery in this book, but there are many ways to start educating with the virtues. The virtues in the books by Linda Kavelin Popov are listed alphabetically from Assertiveness to Unity. It is obviously not necessary to follow that order. I began with the virtue 'patience' because its description inspired me.

I usually suggest to parents in my courses that they can start by paying attention to virtues shown by their family members: "You're good at this, although you might take that for granted ... By naming virtues instead of just saying 'Well done' or 'Good boy', you start developing a positive loop, and you can then use this to develop other virtues; virtues that might be more challenging for you and which require a bit more attention. You can practice your already well-developed virtues to support you in this process."

It would of course be great if your family wants to walk the virtues path with you, but unfortunately this is not always the case. Never mind! You can always start by focusing on a particular virtue yourself. For instance you could read a virtues card every day or week and reflect on it. If you try and practice a virtue yourself, you will see that your family members will start paying attention. Especially if you explain to them how you practice a virtue and how it benefits you.

It's best not to try to recognize, acknowledge and practice all virtues at once. Becoming aware of the virtues is a gradual process. So do not give up if educating with virtues doesn't go well at first. Remember that it is never too late to develop virtues, what matters is to open yourself up to it. Give yourself and your children time: this goal is only reached by small steps. Patience, love and enthusiasm helped me at the beginning. I was completely amazed about the number of virtues I could acknowledge in Daniel, even when he was only two years old. Discipline helped me to persevere: I know creating new habits takes time and effort, and that daily practice really helps me progress. The virtue of moderation helped me not to overdo it with 'determination' and 'excellence'. Not that there's anything wrong with those wonderful qualities!

Sometimes it is hard to find the virtues in your children. You might be wondering: "Am I stupid?" or "Am I a bad dad or mom?" But maybe you should ask yourself: "Have I had time for myself lately? What do I need to recharge my own battery?" A clear vision and optimism are definitely helped by having a fully charged battery yourself.

What are virtues?

Master Facilitator Willy Hensen describes a virtue as your inner tendency to do the right thing. Linda Kavelin Popov calls it a quality of the soul. The interplay of virtues results in an overall attitude.
Practicing these provides us with knowledge of what is good, for ourselves and others, and in different situations. The virtues are like your inner compass. The Virtues Project invites you to reflect on these virtues and to act from them. Using the virtues approach, parents can guide their children in a constructive and positive way to make moral decisions, and where needed help them to correct these.

Are all virtues good?

A virtue is never on its own or without a context. Being determined in your action is brilliant if it happens with respect for others and with consideration. Patience is a great virtue when interacting with others, but not when you have an appointment to keep. In that case purposefulness might be more effective. Always being assertive is usually not appreciated. However, it can be if it is in the right situation. Obedience is acceptable if the person asking for it intends something good and is respectful and caring to you. But we don't want our children to become servile 'yes-men'. In other words, the context determines if you practice a certain virtue or not. You choose depending on the situation or need. A virtue is therefore never seen without the context in which it is applied. If and how you practice a virtue is also determined by your cultural background.

Many of the interludes in this book deal with this aspect because it was one of my biggest discoveries. Check out for instance the paragraph 'The virtue is in the middle' on page 28 and the exercise with the virtues scale on page 142.

How many and which virtues are there?

People often ask: "Why is humor not on the list? That surely is a virtue." The list of virtues on page 187 is not complete. Dan Popov - husband of the author Linda Kavelin Popov and co-founder of the Virtues Project - found more than 300 virtues in the holy writings of all world religions. You will see virtues everywhere if you pay attention: in magazines, newspapers, adverts and on television. Our society is based on them, whether we have been raised or live in a religious environment or not.

Some descriptions of virtues are very similar. They have nearly the same meaning; they just vary in small ways. You can add more virtues to the list of virtues.

You will find virtues in this book that are not on the virtues list. Our family has discovered phrases and expressions that assisted our understanding of specific virtues or their use in specific contexts.
Do feel free to make the virtues approach your own by using your own creativity.

Wish to react?

I have had many positive reactions to the first two Dutch editions of this book. I cherish the opportunity to learn from personal experiences of - for instance - other parents or teachers. Please share these with me by email: info@actonvirtues.nl. Please mention if you give me permission to use your comments on my website or in a newsletter.

About the author

Annelies Wiersma is one of the founding members of the Virtues Project™ - in the Netherlands. She laid her hands on *The Family Virtues Guide* by Linda Kavelin Popov in 2001. She became immediately enthusiastic about the virtues approach, did a Facilitator Training with Margeret Mohamed and Sue Ferguson at Geneva and introduced the virtues approach in her family and in her work as a communication trainer.

Annelies supported the Dutch publications of the Virtues Project. She has been the chair of the Dutch Virtues Project (Stichting Virtues Project Nederland) since 2004. Annelies owns her own business ACT on Virtues and has been giving advice, coaching and training since 2002 about the five strategies of the Virtues Project to parents and schools, both in the Netherlands and abroad (Belgium, Denmark). Next to her training and practical experience as a communication trainer, Annelies has worked as journalist and textwriter. She publicizes regularly about the Virtues Project, for instance in Dutch magazines.

ACT on Virtues also publicizes other virtues books and materials in Dutch including A Pace of Grace and a set of 100 virtues reflection cards (both from Linda Kavelin Popov) and The Advetures of Mali & Keela (Jonathan Collins).

Linda Kavelin Popov has given Annelies the honorary title Master Facilitator for her work with the virtues. As Master Facilitator Annelies provides training and mentoring to new facilitators who want to work with groups with the Virtues Project.

About the illustrator

Carlien Dubben has been illustrating this book. Carlien and Annelies were classmates on highschool and met eachother again after nearly twenty years, by coincendence, just when Annelies started writing *Raising children with virtues*.

Carlien also illustrated a lot of colouring pictures from animals showing virtues. They are all available as free downloads on the website www.actonvirtues.nl

Besides working as an illustrator Carlien also makes monotypes, sjablon pressings and linoleum cuts. She is currently working with woodcuts. Her work is excibited reguarly.

List of 52 virtues*

Assertiveness
Caring
Cleanliness
Commitment
Compassion
Compassion
Confidence
Consideartion
Cooperation
Courage
Courtesy
Creativity
Detachment
Determination
Diligence
Enthusiasm
Excellence
Flexibility
Forgiveness
Friendliness
Generosity
Gentleness
Helpfulness
Honesty
Humility
Idealism

Integrity
Joyfulness
Justice
Kindness
Love
Loyalty
Moderation
Modesty
Orderliness
Patience
Peacefulness
Perseverance
Purposefulness
Reliability
Respect
Responsibility
Self-disciopline
Service
Tact
Thankfulness
Tolerance
Trust
Trustworthiness
Trustfulness
Understanding
Unity

* This list is from The Virtues Projec™ Educator's Guide

THE SPIRITUAL COMPANIONING PROCESS

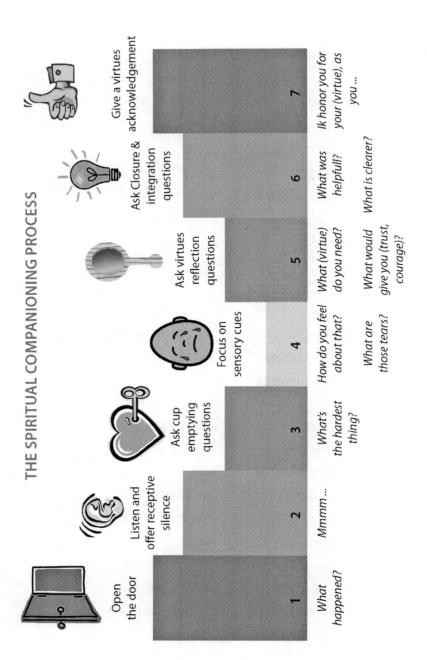

1	2	3	4	5	6	7
Open the door	Listen and offer receptive silence	Ask cup emptying questions	Focus on sensory cues	Ask virtues reflection questions	Ask Closure & integration questions	Give a virtues acknowledgement
What happened?	*Mmmm ...*	*What's the hardest thing?*	*How do you feel about that?*	*What (virtue) do you need?*	*What was helpful!?*	*Ik honor you for your (virtue), as you ...*
			What are those tears?	*What would give you (trust, courage)?*	*What is clearer?*	

The companion follows   The companion leads

9995141R0011

Made in the USA
Charleston, SC
30 October 2011